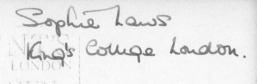

MARTIN HENGEL

Property and Riches in the Early Church

Aspects of a Social History of Early Christianity

SCM PRESS LTD

REGENT'S
UNIVERSITY LONDON

For Karl Heinrich Rengstorf
on his sixtieth birthday

Translated by John Bowden from the German
Eigentum und Reichtum in der frühen Kirche,
published 1973 by Calwer Verlag, Stuttgart

334 01329 1

First British edition 1974
published by SCM Press Ltd
56 Bloomsbury Street, London

Typeset by Specialised Offset Services Ltd, Liverpool
and printed in Great Britain by
Butler & Tanner Ltd, Frome

Contents

Preface

This study goes back to a lecture which I gave in Tutzing in June 1972 to an audience of Bavarian lawyers on the theme of 'Property in the New Testament'. Even then I was convinced that this theme, like the description of ethical preaching throughout the New Testament, needed to be extended into the early church. A much abbreviated version, in the form of theses, appeared in the January 1973 volume of the *Evangelischen Kommentare*.

It seems to me that in today's discussion of theology and ethics there is a need to rethink completely the fellowship and the self-understanding of the early church in the earliest period. Even in a much altered world this could be of exemplary significance for a Christianity which does not know which way to turn and which, in a minority status, must again reflect on its particular spiritual calling. Only by reflecting on its origin will it achieve sufficient authority also to be able to give convincing answers in social and political questions. The 'minority situation' of Christians today brings with it a twofold danger. Either Christians will cut themselves off from the world, as a sect, or they will lend themselves to misuse at the hands of changing political and secular forces as the result of a collaborationist policy. Neither possibility excludes the danger of a political Pharisaism. Only a self-critical examination of the history of Christianity, and particularly of its origins, can protect us from these dangers. Even the 'Christian social ethics' which is so fashionable today must pay more attention to the foundations of the

social history of early Christianity if it is to remain a
'Christian' social ethics. It should not expect to take over a
ready-made programme from early Christianity, but it will
receive basic impulses for its own belief and action.

This brief work sets out to be no more than a general
introduction. It is meant to act as a stimulus to further study,
i.e. to concern with the sources themselves. Every single
chapter really needs a monograph to itself, and the author is
well aware of the limitations of his study, especially as it
covers areas which extend well beyond his own specialist
knowledge. However, the mere attempt to provide an
introductory survey has been both stimulating and instruc-
tive.

I am particularly grateful to my assistant, Herr Klaus W.
Müller, for his help in obtaining literature and checking the
manuscript.

Tübingen, July 1973

1

The Criticism of Property among the Fathers, Natural Law and Utopia in Antiquity

1 The Criticism of Property among the Fourth-Century Fathers

People today are fond of talking about the 'crisis of private property'. Yet this 'crisis' seems to be as old as mankind itself. One might almost say that it is of the 'essence' of mankind, which is always 'in crisis'. In an early Christian romance, the so-called Pseudo-Clementines (*Hom*.3,25), the name of the first fratricide, Cain, is defined on the basis of a double Hebrew etymology, as 'possession' (from *qana* = acquire) and 'envy' (from *qana'* = be envious). It is explained that as a result Cain became a 'murderer' and a 'liar'. From this follows the terse and radical conclusion: 'For all men, possessions are sins' (*pasi ta ktemata hamartemata*, 15.9). An old Hellenistic-Jewish tradition probably stands behind the connection of Cain with possessions; we shall find it again in Philo the philosopher and Josephus the historian. The latter stresses that in his wickedness Cain 'was only concerned to acquire possessions and was the first to plough the earth', in other words, he was the first to acquire land and do violence to nature (*Antt*.1,52; cf. Philo, *Sac.Ab. et C*.1,2). This idea that private property is a root of human dissension goes through the social admonitions of the fathers of the early church like a scarlet thread. The struggle for individual possessions destroys the original good order of the world, as all had an equal share in God's gifts. The greatest Christian preacher of antiquity, John Chrysostom (354-407), puts this view in a particularly impressive way:

> Mark the wise dispensation of God! That he might put mankind to shame, he has made certain things common, as

the sun, air, earth, and water . . . whose benefits are dispensed equally to all as brethren . . . observe, that concerning things that are common there is no contention, but all is peaceable. But when one attempts to possess himself of anything, to make it his own, then contention is introduced, as if nature herself were indignant, that when God brings us together in every way, we are eager to divide and separate ourselves by appropriating things, and by using those cold words 'mine and thine'. Then there is contention and uneasiness. But where this is not, no strife or contention is bred. This state therefore is rather our inheritance, and more agreeable to nature.[1]

The judgment of the rather older monastic father Basil (329-379) was hardly less radical. He himself came from a family of rich landowners in Asia Minor and after his studies distributed all his possessions among the poor, influenced by the radical asceticism of the monks of Egypt (see pp.52f. below). He preached a famous sermon on the rich farmer (Luke 12.18) in which he called the man who could help the needy but keeps his possessions to himself a 'robber and a thief'. At the same time he gives a clear answer to the objection of the hard-hearted man who asks, 'To whom am I doing wrong . . . if I keep my possessions to myself?'

Tell me, what is yours? Where did you get it and bring it into the world? It is as if one has taken a seat in the theatre and then drives out all who come later, thinking that what is for everyone is only for him. Rich people are like that. For having pre-empted what is common to all, they make it their own by virtue of this prior possession. If only each one would take as much as he requires to satisfy his immediate needs, and leave the rest to others who equally needed it, no one would be rich — and no one would be poor (Migne, PG 31, 276f.).

Here the great Cappadocian is taking up imagery which had already been used by Chrysippus, head of the school of Stoic philosophers (*c*.280-207 BC), though he slants it in a polemical direction. The Stoic had wanted to defend 'the right to private property' by reference to a seat at the theatre which is occupied by the first arrival, as it 'does not militate against the state or the universe which are common to all'.[2] Basil holds exactly the opposite view. As Bishop of Caesarea in Cappadocia, he tried to translate his social demands into action by setting up a large welfare centre at the gates of the city for the poor, the old and the sick, together with a hospice for penniless travellers. Refuges of this kind also came into being in other cities in his diocese.

His friend and contemporary Gregory Nazianzen gave this criticism of property and riches a grounding in salvation history and doctrine: poverty and superfluity, so-called freedom and slavery are a consequence of the Fall. 'In the beginning it was not so': God created man 'free and independent'. He was rich, for the goods of paradise were freely at his disposal. The 'envy and quarrelsomeness' of the serpent first destroyed the original harmony and 'shattered the nobility of nature through covetousness, with the help of despotic laws'. Works of righteousness and mercy are therefore an essential step towards the restoration of this lost state.[3] This thesis that private property came into being as a result of the Fall had great influence in the history of the church. We find it later among the Franciscan theologians and then again in Zwingli and Melanchthon. The later devaluation of property, the thesis that it has only secondary character by contrast with an original equality, also in essentials goes back to this derivation of private property from the Fall.

2   Natural Law and Utopia in Antiquity

Of course, 'theories of property' like this, which are to be found in the early church, are not specifically based on the New Testament. Appeal could be made equally well to philosophy and natural law for the thesis of Gregory Nazianzen that private property, riches and poverty are a consequence of the Fall. Thus we find Ambrose, Bishop of Milan (339-397), arguing against Cicero (*De off*.1.20ff.) but agreeing with Stoic teaching:

> Nature has poured forth all things for men for common use. God has ordered all things to be produced, so that there should be food in common to all, and that the earth

should be a common possession for all. Nature, therefore, has produced a common right for all, but greed (*usurpatio*) had made it a right for a few.[7]

This fundamental idea, that in the 'golden age', i.e. in the primal childhood of the human race, all possessions were held in common – even to the point of sharing wives – and that the moral downfall of man began with the introduction of private property, dominates much of ancient 'philosophy of history' and the utopian states influenced by it. Here ancient natural law, the philosophy of history and the Christian doctrine of man's primal state could join hands. Aristophanes could already present utopias of this kind as feminine wisdom in a comedy about an early agitator for women's liberation. The future and the ideal world will again correspond:

All shall be equal, and equally share
all wealth and enjoyment, nor longer endure
that one should be rich, and another be poor,
that one should have acres, far stretching and wide,
and another not even enough to provide
himself with a grave: that this at his call
should have hundreds of servants and that none at all.
All this I intend to correct and amend:
now all of all blessings shall freely partake,
one life and one system for all men I'll make.[5]

Behind these demands, which sound familiar to us today, stands the romantic regression of 'back to nature', which played an astonishing role in the thought of the intellectuals of antiquity. It was a widely-accepted commonplace that the first men lived in a state of perfect moral innocence, without any external laws, and directed only by 'nature':

Golden was that first age, which, with no one to compel, without a law, of its own will, kept faith and did the right. There was no fear of punishment, no threatening words were to be read on brazen tablets; no suppliant throng gazed fearfully upon its judge's face; but without judges lived secure.[6]

This 'ideal state' was only possible because 'private property' was as unknown as the seductive skills of technology; men lived without any needs whatsoever on what the earth produced generously and without compulsion, acorns, roots and wild fruits:

> Even to mark the field or divide it with bounds was unlawful. Men made gain from the common store, and Earth yielded all, of herself, more freely, when none begged for her gifts.[7]

Obviously, the 'lordship of men over men' was also completely absent, and with it all forms of slavery. This paradisal condition was only destroyed by the introduction of technical means, metal working, agriculture which violated the earth, various forms of craft, voyaging and trade: done violence to by men, nature began to withhold itself. Covetousness, envy, tyranny and war raised their ugly heads and began to darken man's common life.

Still people continued to believe that they would rediscover the lost ideal of the time of paradise, long past, among individual barbarian peoples. Attention was especially fixed on the Scythians, who were regarded as being particularly wild: they were supposed to live almost like animals, but on the other hand supreme moral perfection was attributed to them:

> They are frugal in their ways of living and not money-getters, they not only are orderly towards one another, because they have all things in common (*koina panta echontes*, cf. Acts 2.44, see pp.8f., 31ff. below), their wives, children, the whole of their kin and everything, but also remain invincible and unconquered by others, because they have nothing to be enslaved for.[8]

Another possibility was to tell stories of distant isles of wonder in utopian romances. One instance of this is the famous romance of Euhemerus which tells of the island Panchaea in the Indian Ocean. The whole island was held in common and there was a strict duty to hand over all agricultural products. Fair portions were given 'to each according to his need', though incentives for particular assiduity were not lacking. There was no private property apart from 'house and garden'; the 'intellectual groups', i.e. the wise priests, saw to just laws and distribution. The analogy to Plato's philosophers' state is unmistakable (Diod.5,45,3-5).

It is, of course, striking that the Greeks and Romans hardly thought about a future utopia, the return of the golden age. The agitation in Aristophanes' *Ecclesiazousae* is an exception. Under the influence of the oriental-Jewish Sibyls, that is of apocalyptic, Virgil is the first to proclaim the dawn of future salvation, in his much-discussed fourth Eclogue:

> Every land shall bear all fruits. The earth shall not feel the harrow, nor the vine the pruning hook; the sturdy ploughman, too, shall now loose his oxen from the yoke.[9]

When the earth once again offers its gifts in abundance, and without being violated by man's techniques, there will no longer be any need for private property. The time of the great peace has dawned.

Ideals of this kind gave wing to romantic longing more than to real hope, though at the same time they also inspired the moral preaching of the philosophers. Thus Seneca, the Roman Stoic and Nero's tutor, could already speak in very similar terms to the later church father Gregory Nazianzen:

> (Philosophy) has taught us to worship that which is divine, to love that which is human; she has told us that with the gods lies dominion, and among men, fellowship. This fellowship remained unspoiled for a long time, until avarice tore the community asunder and became the cause of poverty even in the case of those whom she herself had most enriched. For men cease to possess all things the moment they desire all things for their own. But the first men and those who sprang from them, still unspoiled, followed nature (*Epist*.90.3f.).

> But avarice broke in upon a condition so happily ordained, and, by its eagerness to lay something away and to turn it to its own private use, made all things the property of others, and reduced itself from boundless wealth to straitened need. It was avarice that introduced

poverty, and, by craving much, lost all (*Epist*.90.38).[10]

This means that the utopia projected back into primal times, the doctrine of the original state of paradise and the fall that followed, which is said to have consisted not least in the appropriation of private property, is by no means a genuinely Christian doctrine. Rather, it is a mythical specu- lation about history which was widespread in antiquity.

The connections between the ancient theories of a lofty moral 'primal communism' or of a 'primal catastrophe', allegedly introduced by the division of labour and private possessions, and the modern 'historical myths' of popular Marxism, are evident. Rousseau's 'back to nature', like Proudhon's theory 'property is theft', are not original ideas, but go back to ancient sources.

Even the view that particular people in the South Sea Islands and the primeval Brazilian forest enjoy economic and sexual innocence, or that the 'hunters and collectors' with their primal communism had ideal social conditions, corres- ponds to a widespread ancient myth about the just laws of the barbarians. In the beginning, a natural, i.e. morally perfect condition is said to have prevailed. A fundamentally religious longing for the 'good old days' underlies these universal ancient doctrines of man's primal state, which can also be found in different variations in Iranian, Babylonian, Indian and indeed Chinese myths.[11] Then, it was believed, the world was whole. Of course, there is no historical proof of this and it is certainly no more rational than hope for an eternal life in the Elysian fields or on the isles of the blessed.

However, these myths of the primal state of man were rarely evaluated in political terms. Pressure for imposing a utopian pattern on the present and future is most likely to be found where one may conjecture a connection with Jewish and oriental apocalyptic (see pp.17ff. below), say in Aristonicus' rebellion in the Pergamene kingdom (133-130 BC). After handing over the country to Rome, he 'quickly assembled a mass of poor people and slaves who were summoned to freedom and whom he named Heliopolitans'. Presumably he was striving for a utopian 'proletarian state', to which he gave the name 'sun state'.[12] The Egyptian Potter's Oracle, which was similarly composed in the second century BC, has many features in common with the Jewish apocalypses. Together with the expulsion of the Greeks from Egypt and the destruction of Alexandria there is also a prophecy of the liberation of the slaves, 'whose masters flee for their life', after the upheaval.[13] The concerns of the ancient social reformers hardly went beyond a demand for the liberation of slaves, remission of debts and a redistribution of agricultural land. Here the strongest social impetus came from the Jewish heritage (see pp.15ff. below). By contrast, the influence of philosophical utopia on political reality was relatively small; the popular philosophical, utopian romance of the state hardly had any concrete effect. There were exceptions, e.g. when the Stoic Sphaerus supported the Spartan king Agis IV in his radical social reform,[14] or when the philosopher Blossius, who was hostile to Rome, fled to Aristonicus at Pergamon. There was no 'ideological' foundation to the great slave revolts of the Hellenistic period between the third and first centuries BC.

3   Greek Influence in Early Christianity?

Early Christianity and the New Testament, the 'documentation of the preaching on which the church was founded' (M. Kähler) and thus the earliest source of Christian history, were only marginally affected by all these theories and utopias, which gave their stamp to later Christian natural law theory about property. A conjunction of the primitive Christian ethos and the universal ideal of antiquity was most likely to come about where a New Testament author — like Luke — introduced his Greek rhetorical training as a writer and stylized certain phenomena of early Christianity in accordance with the tradition in which he had been educated. This is the case, for example, with the account which Luke gives of the so-called communism of the first community in Jerusalem:

> And all who believed were together and had all things in common (Acts 2.44). Now the company of those who believed were of one heart and soul, and no one said that any of the things which he possessed was his own, but they had everything in common (*panta koina*: Acts 4.32).

Here we have the familiar picture of the restoration of the
perfect 'primal state' which has analogies, even to the way in
which it is formulated, with the sharing of goods among the
Scythians (see p.5 above), Plato's doctrine of the state
(*Pol.*462, etc.) or the 'primal community' of the Pythagoreans in Southern Italy.[15] The *Sentences of Sextus* which,
while Christian, are also fed from popular Pythagorean
philosophical sources (see below, pp.56f.), give a theological
foundation to this ideal, which both Christians and pagans
could accept. 'Those who have in common God as their
Father, but do not have possessions in common, are
impious.'[16] A still nearer parallel to Luke's account is the
'community of goods' among the Essene groups in Palestine,
above all in their centre at Qumran, which we can see
particularly well as a result of the discovery of the Dead Sea
Scrolls. But even here we must ask whether this 'group
communism', with its eschatological stamp, which also made
a vivid impression on the educated Graeco-Roman world
outside Palestine, was not shaped as much by the ideals of
the Hellenistic spirit of the age as by Old Testament patterns.
The Essenes wanted to realize here on earth a perfect — one
might almost say 'angelic' or 'heavenly' — form of community through the ideal of the sharing of goods. They lived
in the awareness that they were in constant contact with the
angels of God, and their aim was to regain the original rank
and glory of the primal man Adam (1 QS 4.23; 1 QH 17.15).
The other side of this exaggerated estimation of themselves
was that they regarded the rest of mankind, their Jewish
contemporaries and still more the Gentiles, as a 'mass of
corruption', as sons of darkness delivered over to annihilation. These people were to be hated eternally until they were
completely annihilated in the 'last combat' (1 QS 1.10; 9.21).

There are considerably stronger points of contact between
New Testament criticism of property and riches and that of
the Graeco-Roman world in the sphere of popular wisdom.
Thus in the late I Timothy 6.10 we find a widespread
proverb, 'The love of money is the root of all evils', cited in
connection with a demand for pious 'self-sufficiency'
(*autarkeia*), i.e. the 'favourite virtue of Cynics and Stoics'.[17]
This in turn influenced the later Christian tradition. This

saying expresses a principal theme of popular philosophical preaching, and an ever-increasing number of variations on it are quoted in ancient sources.[18] An especially favourite version can be found equally in the sage Democritus and in Diogenes, who despised both culture and possessions: 'The love of money is the homeland of all evils'.[19] But the saying is not lacking in Jewish-Hellenistic literature either.[20] Here we have a good example of the way in which popular-philosophical criticism of avarice and riches could be combined with Judaeo-Christian 'social criticism' in the sphere of ethical admonitions.

Finally, an example may be quoted which points forward to the teaching of Jesus.

In the 'Misanthrope' (*Dyskolos*), written by the Attic comedian Menander (born 342/1 BC), the young Sostratus delivers a vigorous moral sermon to his father when the latter is bitter at the thought of a poor cousin marrying into his rich family:

> That's a bit thick!
> I do not want to be father-in-law of
> two penniless children. One is quite enough.

The son rejoins:

> You babble about money, a matter insecure. For if you
> have knowledge that this will abide with you for ever, keep
> it close, share it with none, but be yourself its lord and
> master. Whereas if you possess all this, not as your own
> but Fortune's, why should you, father, begrudge it to
> anyone of these? For she herself perhaps, taking all this
> away from you, will bestow it in turn on someone else
> who is unworthy. Wherefore I say that you yourself, what
> time you are the master, ought to use this nobly, father,
> ought to succour all and through your help effect that as
> many as possible should live in easy circumstances. For
> this is something that will never die, and, if reverses some
> day befall you, from this source you in turn will have the
> self-same help. A visible friend is a better thing by far than
> wealth which you keep buried out of sight.[21]

H. Hommel has pointed to a series of parallels between

these verses and the synoptic gospels and the preaching of Jesus.[22] The theme that one should exchange the uncertain, threatened and transitory possession of property for the permanence of friendship which will recompense good deeds in future need can be found, for example, in the Lukan special material as an interpretation of the difficult parable of the unjust steward: 'And I tell you, make friends for yourselves by means of unrighteous mammon, so that when it fails they may receive you into the eternal habitations' (16.9). There is also a parallel in the favourite theme of 'disappearing riches', which occurs above, to the saying from the Sermon on the Mount; 'Lay up for yourselves treasures in heaven, where neither moth nor rust consumes and where thieves do not break in and steal' (Matt. 6.20 = Luke 12.35). On the other hand, one should not, of course, overlook the fact that in the gospel sayings the eschatological reference is fundamentally different from the naive experiential wisdom of Greek gnomic thought. Moreover, the whole terminology, for example the formula about 'unrighteous mammon', clearly points to a Jewish-Palestinian derivation. Nevertheless, these more or less chance instances may show how there were mutual links between the Jewish and early Christian criticism of riches on the one hand and that of popular Greek philosophy on the other.

2

Property and Riches in the Old Testament and Judaism

1 The Prophetic Criticism of Riches and its Expression in the Torah

Before we consider the attitude of Jesus and early Christianity to property and riches, we must take a look at the Old Testament and Jewish tradition out of which early Christianity grew. Here the message of the prophets and the social legislation of the Torah had long stimulated criticism of property. The right to property was in principle subordinated to the obligation to care for the weaker members of society. Even the testimony of the first writing prophet, Amos, in the eighth century BC, leaves nothing to be desired by way of clarity. With unsurpassable sharpness he attacks the subjection and exploitation of the poor by the rich landowners and royal officials in the northern kingdom:

> They hate him who reproves in the gate,
> and they abhor him who speaks the truth.
> Therefore:
> Because you trample the poor
> and take from him exactions of wheat,
> you have built houses of hewn stone,
> but you shall not dwell in them.
> You have planted pleasant vineyards,
> but you shall not drink their wine.
> For I know how many are your transgressions,
> and how great are your sins —
> you who afflict the righteous, who take a bribe,
> and turn aside the needy in the gate. (Amos 5.10-12)

Hear this,
you who trample upon the needy,
and bring the poor of the land to an end,
saying,
'When will the new moon be over,
that we may sell grain?
And the sabbath,
that we may offer wheat for sale,
that we may make the ephah small and the shekel great,
and deal deceitfully with false balances,
that we may buy the poor for silver
and the needy for a pair of sandals,
and sell the refuse of the wheat?'
The Lord has sworn by the pride of Jacob:
'Surely I will never forget any of their deeds.
Shall not the land tremble on this account,
and every one mourn who dwells in it?' (Amos 8.4-8)

Amos' threats against society are continued a little later by
Isaiah, in the southern kingdom. He, too, roughly attacks the
dispossession practised by the great landowners, the corruption among the judges and the mercilessness and partiality of
officials:

Woe to those who join house to house,
who add field to field,
until there is no more room,
and you are made to dwell alone in the midst of the land.
The Lord of hosts has sworn in my hearing:
'Surely many houses shall be desolate,
large and beautiful houses, without inhabitant.
For ten acres of vineyard shall yield but one bath,
and a homer of seed shall yield but an ephah. . . .'

Woe to those who decree iniquitous decrees,
and the writers who keep writing oppression,
to turn aside the needy from justice
and to rob the poor of my people of their right,
that widows may be their spoil,
and that they may make the fatherless their prey.
What will you do on the day of punishment,

in the storm which will come from afar?
To whom will you flee for help,
and where will you leave your wealth? (Isa.5.8-10; 10.1-3)

Otto Kaiser refers to the third elegy of the great Athenian lawgiver and social reformer Solon, which was written about a century later. Solon is dealing with a similar situation in his native city:

But the citizens themselves, driven by the desire for money, are blinded and seek the fall of our mighty city.
For the leaders of the people are wicked and evil-minded, and thereby only bring painful suffering upon themselves. Their greed is insatiable, they do not know how to enjoy with order and sobriety the pleasures of the feast.
... The riches they heap up come from violence and wrong; neither what the gods possess nor what belongs to man is spared by their appetite; they are not ashamed of open robbery, have no regard for *dike* (the goddess of righteousness) and her sacred commandment.[1]

At least part of the social message of the prophets was given expression in the Torah, later ascribed to Moses, especially in the book of Deuteronomy, which played a decisive role in king Josiah's reform and in the spiritual renewal of Israel during the exile. Examples of this are the numerous regulations contained in the Torah which protect the weak and underprivileged members of society. In Deut.15.1ff.,12ff., the ordinance of the year of release which takes place every seven years enjoined a universal release of debts and the freeing of all who had been enslaved for debt. The prophet Jeremiah was already protesting against the breach of this practice (34.8ff.). In the fiftieth year, after seven years of release or sabbath years, the 'year of jubilee' was celebrated. In this year all land that had been sold in the meantime was to be returned to its original owner or his heirs (Lev.25.8ff.). The reason given for this 'redistribution' of land was that Yahweh was the real owner of the holy land: 'For the land is mine; for you are strangers and sojourners with me' (Lev.25.23). 'Each of you shall return to his property'(25.13). 'What is called a sale is not really a sale; it is merely a provisional exchange of possessions; for Yahweh alone is the owner of the land. The Israelites are merely hereditary tenants on his property, who have no more ultimate right to dispose of the land which had been assigned to them than the strangers and sojourners whom they have accepted in their midst.'[2] We find the three demands for the remission of debt, the freeing of slaves and the redistribution of land in numerous attempts at social reform in the ancient world: the Jewish law attempted to institutionalize these ever-recurring basic demands of 'ancient social reform', though of course it remains an open question how far the demands were ever realized. Significantly enough, the 'year of jubilee' was later reinterpreted as a symbol of the eschatological liberation of Israel.

On the other side was appropriate and legitimate possession under the protection of the Decalogue, which prohibited envious covetousness of a neighbour's property (Ex.20.15,17 = Deut.5.19,21). The picture of the king's peace in the time of Solomon, when 'Judah and Israel dwelt in safety, every man under his vine and under his fig tree' (I Kings 4.25), became a symbol of the prophetic vision of the time of salvation (Micah 4.4; Zech. 3.10; cf. also II Kings 18.31).

2   Social Tensions in Early Judaism

The contrast between the great landowners and the small peasant farmers or landless tenants had already led to considerable social tensions in the late monarchy (I Kings 21; Isa.5.8ff.; Micah 2.2) and then again in the Persian period under Nehemiah (5.1ff.). The situation became considerably more acute in the Hellenistic period after Alexander, as the Graeco-Macedonian colonizers with their own particular approach to the world went over from the extensive exploitation hitherto usual in the East to an intensive exploitation of their subject territories. The Romans and the rulers appointed by them, like Herod and his successors, continued this form of extreme exploitation of the land. Great estates forced back the free peasant farmers, and the number of landless tenants increased, particularly after the time of Herod. We have a lively picture of the social scene in Palestine from the parables of Jesus with their landowners, tenants, day labourers and slaves; with faithful and unfaithful administrators; with remission of debts and slavery for debts. The social scene has the firm imprint of feudalism upon it. We can understand why the Jewish struggles for freedom — first of all that of the Maccabees against the Macedonian Seleucids and then later that of the 'Zealots' against the Romans — were always also social struggles. When the Jewish rebels plundered Jerusalem in AD 66 from their base in the temple, the first thing that they burnt was the city archive with the land-registers and the accounts of debts (Josephus, *Bell*.2,427). Later, Simon bar Giora, the leader of the Zealots, arranged for a general liberation of slaves (4,508). Josephus particularly stresses that the rebellion was supported above all by the simple people — and the youth — whereas the upper classes sought to maintain peace with Rome.[3]

Thus there was a political and a social division not only in Palestinian Judaism, but also in large areas of the Diaspora, e.g. in Egypt and in Cyrenaica. This rift also goes through many parts of the religious tradition. For example, on the eve of the Hellenistic reform, which led on to the Maccabean revolt (*c*. 180 BC), the wisdom teacher Ben Sira uttered polemic against unscrupulous speculators and against the hectic hunt for riches:

> My son, do not busy yourself with many matters; if you
>   multiply activities you will not go unpunished
>   (Sir.11.10).
> He who loves gold will not be justified,
> and he who pursues money will be led astray to it
> (Ecclus.31.5).

Rich and poor act like the wolf and the lamb; the gulf between them is unbridgeable:

> A rich man does wrong, and he even adds reproaches;
>   a poor man suffers wrong and he must add apologies.
> A rich man will exploit you if you can be of use to him,
>   but if you are in need he will forsake you (13.3f.).

> Wild asses in the wilderness are the prey of lions;
>   likewise the poor are pastures for the rich.

Humility is an abomination to a proud man;
  likewise a poor man is an abomination to a rich one.
When a rich man totters, he is steadied by friends,
  but when a humble man falls, he is even pushed away by
  friends (13.19ff.).

Ben Sira's polemic against social injustice at times becomes
even as sharp as the preaching of the prophets:

Like one who kills a son before his father's eyes
  is the man who offers a sacrifice from the property of
  the poor.
The bread of the needy is the life of the poor;
  whoever deprives them of it is a man of blood.
To take away a neighbour's living is to murder him;
  to deprive an employee of his wages is to shed blood
  (34.20-22).

But this is only one side of the coin. On the other side we
find in immediate juxtaposition in Ben Sira the high
estimation of riches which is to be found in traditional
wisdom: riches gained through honest work and God's
blessing guarantee a safe and carefree life, whereas self-
incurred poverty and beggary are hateful to him.[4] It is
certainly no coincidence that Ben Sira praises the just rich
man rather than the poor man:

Blessed is the rich man who is found blameless and who
does not go after mammon (Sir.31.8).

We shall look in vain for direct praise of the poor or of
poverty in Jewish literature: it is first to be found in the
gospel (Luke 6.20, see below, p.25).

The apocalyptic threat of judgment against the unjust rich
is all the sharper. Thus we read in the admonitions of
Ethiopian Enoch:

Woe to those who build unrighteousness and oppression
And lay deceit as a foundation;
For they shall be suddenly overthrown,
And they shall have no peace (cf. Isa.48.22; 57.21).
Woe to those who build their houses with sin;
For from all their foundations shall they be overthrown,

And by the sword they shall fall.
And those who acquire gold and silver in judgment shall
   suddenly perish.
Woe to you, ye rich, for ye have trusted in your riches,
And from your riches shall ye depart,
Because ye have not remembered the Most High in the
   days of your riches.
Ye have committed blasphemy and unrighteousness,
And have become ready for the day of slaughter,
And the day of darkness and the day of the great
   judgment.
Thus I speak and declare unto you:
He who created you will overthrow you,
And for your fall there shall be no compassion,
And your Creator will rejoice at your destruction (94.6-10,
   cf. 96.4ff.).
Woe to you who acquire silver and gold in unrighteousness
   and say:
We have become rich with riches and have possessions;
And have acquired everything we have desired.
And now let us do what we purposed:
For we have gathered silver in our treasuries
And many possessions in our houses . . .
You deceive yourselves, for your riches do not abide
But speedily ascend from you;
For ye have acquired it all in unrighteousness (97.8-10, cf.
   100.6).

God's last judgment brings about the great reversal: the rich,
the powerful and the exploiters are given over to eternal
damnation (102.9ff.; cf. 63.10), whereas the faithful and
righteous poor who have 'toiled laboriously' (103.9) all their
lives receive eternal reward. There is no mistaking the fact
that behind the threats and description of judgment a crude
desire for vengeance on the part of the faithful, who have so
far been suppressed, can also be seen. According to the
Similitudes in Ethiopian Enoch 63.10, 'the mighty and the
kings who possess the earth' must confess: 'Our souls are full
of unrighteous mammon (see Luke 16.9,11), but it does not
prevent us from descending from the midst thereof into the
burden of the flame of Sheol.' There 'they shall be a

spectacle for the righteous and . . . elect; they shall rejoice over them, because the wrath of the Lord of Spirits resteth upon them' (62.12). The tradition which emerges here, of the pious feasting their eyes on the torments of hell, can be traced through later Christian apocalyptic down to Dante's Inferno (see below, pp.49f). Behind these threats of judgment there is an earlier Jewish tradition which already appears in the canonical psalms and then is developed by the Essene texts of Qumran and the Pharisaic Psalms of Solomon: the term 'poor' (*'ani* or the related *'anaw* = humble, and *'ebyon*) becomes almost synonymous with 'pious' and 'righteous'. For example, an Essene commentary on Ps.37.10, 'But the humble (*'anawim*) shall possess the land and delight in abundant peace' interprets the text as: '(The congregation of the) Poor (*'ebyonim*) who shall accept the season of penance and shall be delivered from all the snares (of Satan) . . .' In other words, here the Essene community of salvation understands itself to be the 'poor'.[5] According to the War Scroll the hostile nations are conquered 'by the poor', for God himself will 'deliver into the hands of the poor the enemies from all the lands'.[6] Here the eschatological, true Israel is in principle identical with 'the poor'. The term has changed from the designation of a social group to that of a religious group. The early church in Palestine later uses the term 'poor' (*'ebyonim*) to describe itself in a very similar sense (see below, p.34).

3   Poverty and Riches in the Rabbis

Jewish piety which took its stamp from the message of the prophets and the social commandments of the Torah did its utmost to eliminate or at least to alleviate the particularly abrupt contrast between rich and poor in the Hellenistic Roman period. According to a fundamental rule ascribed to the Jewish high priest Simon the Just (200 BC), 'the world stands on three things: on the Torah, and on the Service, and on the doing of kindnesses' (Pirke Aboth 1,2). Later rabbis made a distinction between the so-called 'works of love', like visiting the sick, giving hospitality to strangers, equipping poor betrothed couples, comforting the bereaved, etc., and organized welfare for the poor, but the whole complex could

be summed up as 'good works' (cf. Matt.5.16;
Bill.4.536,559). The redemption of Jewish slaves, which was
particularly important in the Diaspora, must also be included
in this complex of 'works of love'. An early rabbinic maxim
may clarify the high opinion of these works of mercy, which
did much to alleviate social distress:

> Acts of kindness (*gemiloth hasadim*) and charity weigh
> more than all the commandments. Charity can be given to
> the living only, acts of kindness can be done to both the
> living and the dead; charity can be given only to the poor,
> acts of kindness to the rich and the poor. Charity can be
> done only with one's money, but acts of kindness can be
> done with one's person and one's money.[7]

The religious justification of genorisity stressed on the one
hand the idea of 'imitating the goodness of God', which was
equally favoured by Stoic philosophers and rabbis, and on
the other the Old Testament argument, which reappears in
Christian parenesis, that all good gifts come from God
himself. Thus R. Eleazar b. Judah, about AD 100, remarked:

> Give him (i.e. God) of what is his, for thou and thine are
> his. And thus (the Scripture) saith, in (the place concern-
> ing) David, 'For all things come of thee, and of thine own
> have we given thee' (Aboth 3,7; Bill.4,541).

Consequently the Jewish communities developed a system of
welfare for the poor which was probably unique in antiquity
(before the rise of Christianity) and extremely effective. The
legal basis for it was the second tithe, the so-called tithe for
the poor, commanded in Deut.14.29; 26.12. Of course, at
this point we can also see the limitations of this institution.
Radical criticism of riches and surrender of one's own
resources were taboo among the rabbis; to protect a man
from making himself penniless a limit was put on the amount
of alms to be given to the poor. The most a man was to give
was twenty per cent of his total income; the least, two or
three per cent. A rabbinic tradition reports: 'Once a man
wanted to give away his property, but his friend did not
allow it.'[8] Practical experience underlies this position: the
rigorist must not become a burden on the community at a

later stage and the resources of the people of Israel may not be squandered. Among the rabbis we increasingly find once again the high estimate put on riches and the despising of the poor which were characteristic of early wisdom. The hasidic, apocalyptic way of poverty had only a very limited influence here. Poverty could be regarded as a curse, and reference could be made to Prov.19.15: 'The days of the poor man are evil.'[9] The judgment was:

> 'There is nothing harder in the world than poverty; for it is the hardest of all the sufferings in the world.' Consequently Job prayed: 'Lord, I will accept all the suffering in the world, but not poverty' (*ExR* 31.12; Bill.1,818).

In accordance with this attitude, there was widespread praise of riches. The following statement was attributed to the famous teacher Rabbi Johanan in the third century AD:

> God makes his Shekinah (i.e. his presence) rest only on a strong man, a *rich man*, a wise man and a humble man . . .

At the same time he is said to have justified it from the Bible:

> All the prophets were rich. How do we know that? From Moses, Samuel, Amos (!) and Jonah (*Ned*.38a; Bill.1,826).

Earlier apocalyptic looked for the abolition of poverty in the coming age, and we can understand why:

> And they who have died in grief shall arise in joy,
> And they who were poor for the Lord's sake shall be made rich,
> And they who are put to death for the Lord's sake shall awake to life (Test.Judah 25.4).

But the Babylonian teacher Mar Samuel, head of the school — who was, of course, particularly restrained in his messianic expectation — could refer to Deut.15.11: 'For the poor will never cease out of the land', and assert:

> 'The only difference between this world and the days of the Messiah is that slavery to governments will cease,' in other words, there will still be poverty and the opportunity for good works. The frequent repetition of this view shows how popular it was (Ber.34b etc.; Bill.1,74).

Here we can see a change in the Jewish attitude to riches. It is connected with the rejection of the Jewish apocalyptic way of poverty which after AD 70 fell more and more under the suspicion of being heresy. At first, the early rabbinic tradition can still report the great poverty of individual teachers between the first century BC and the second century AD. Thus Hillel came from Babylon to Jerusalem as a penurious day-labourer and bought access to the school with half of his scanty earnings. R. Akiba came from equally poor surroundings and was first of all a simple shepherd. However, it is significant that the rabbinic tradition stresses that they achieved not only a great reputation but also prosperity. The riches of the family of the patriarch, the descendants of Hillel, were proverbial after the second century. When R. Akiba declared that 'The poverty of the daughter of Jacob is like a red bridle on the neck of a white horse,'[10] he was not praising poverty as such, but simply saying that Israel was to be brought to repentance by extreme distress. The fearful catastrophes of the Jewish War and the rebellion of Bar Cochba (AD 66-74 and 132-135), which also broke out for social reasons, had brought such profound economic distress on the people that its religious, national and economic existence was threatened. Poverty no longer seemed to be an ideal to be striven for; it was simply God's chastisement. The increasing high estimation of riches and the contempt for poverty among the later teachers is probably connected with the overcoming of this crisis and the strengthening of Judaism towards the end of the second century and in the third century AD. The rabbis had established themselves as the leading religious and political class in Judaism, beyond any question or dispute, and as the acknowledged leaders of the people they had both the possibility and the will to become prosperous. They were opposed to some degree by individual charismatics and miracle workers, whose poverty and extreme asceticism are stressed in legends. Among these were R. Hanina ben Dosa and Abba Hilkiah in the first century, and R. Phinehas b.Jair, the opponent of the immensely rich patriarch Jehuda Hannasi, towards the end of the second century. But these were exceptions which proved the rule.

3

The Preaching of Jesus

What has been said so far indicates that Palestine in the first century AD, at the time of Jesus' ministry and the birth of the early church, was full of acute political, social and religious differences. Evidence for this is provided not least by Josephus and Philo, who report a number of clashes between the Jews and the prefect Pontius Pilate (cf. Luke 13.1f.). The latter was regarded as being particularly avaricious and cruel. The bloody repression of messianic disturbances in Samaria finally led to his dismissal in AD 37 (Josephus, *Antt.* 18,55-64, 85-87; Philo, *Leg. ad C.* 299ff.). This negative picture is supplemented by rabbinic accounts of the avarice and despotism of the leading high-priestly families, among whom pride of place was taken by the house of Annas. This family used their privileged position to exploit those who came to Jerusalem on pilgrimage at festival times and to oppress the more humble ministers of the temple; they often worked hand in hand with the Roman prefects.

1 Jesus' Radical Criticism of Property

We turn first to the synoptic gospels: Mark, Luke and Matthew, which are the main sources about Jesus. In what follows it is impossible to make an exact distinction between what may be supposed to be the authentic tradition about Jesus and its influence on the community tradition of subsequent decades. Cause and effect here are often inextricably fused together.

In contrast to the scriptural learning of the Pharisees, who in their casuistic interpretation of the Torah also concerned themselves intensively with private case law, which to us would seem to belong in the secular sphere, the preaching of Jesus has a quite marked prophetic and religious character. Jesus emerges 'as the one who proclaims and ushers in the coming kingdom of God'.[1] Its dawn is imminent, just about to break, indeed it is already present in a hidden way in the work of Jesus. Thus the demand in the Sermon on the Mount (Matt.6.33) is fundamental to any understanding of his attitude to all earthly goods:

> But seek first the kingdom of God and his righteousness, and all these things shall be yours as well.

For this reason, unlike the scribes, he turns down a request to arbitrate in the case of a disputed legacy:

> Man, who made me a judge or divider over you? (Luke 12.13)

On the contrary, the imminence of the kingdom of God demands freedom over possessions, the renunciation of all care, complete trust in the goodness and providence of the heavenly Father (Matt.6.25-34 = Luke 12.22-32). Service of God and service of mammon are mutually exclusive:

> No one can serve two masters . . . You cannot serve God and mammon (Luke 16.13 = Matt.6.24).

The Aramaic-Phoenician word for possessions or property is clearly used here in a negative sense. Borrowing from contemporary Jewish terminology, the early church could talk directly about 'unrighteous mammon' (Luke 16.19, see above, p.11). Clement of Alexandria supposed that this passage meant that private property was essentially *adikia*, unrighteousness (*Quis dives* 31: GCS 17,180). Perhaps the early church left this Semitic loan-word untranslated because they regarded it almost as the name of an idol: the service of mammon is idolatry. Here possessions acquire a demonic character, because they are a tie to men and close their ears to the summons of the kingdom of God. Jesus' urgent warning against the danger of riches is in accordance with this fundamental criticism. It should be understood against the background of his messianic announcement of the imminence of God, developed in connect with the prophetic pronouncement in Isa.61.1f.:

> The Spirit of the Lord God is upon me,
> because the Lord has anointed me
> to bring good tidings to the poor;
> he has sent me to bind up the broken-hearted,
> to proclaim liberty to the captives
> and the opening of the prison to those who are bound;
> to proclaim the day of the Lord's favour,
> and the day of vengeance of our God;
> to comfort all who mourn;
> to delight those who mourn in Zion.

Luke puts these words in the mouth of Jesus in his first preaching in his home town of Nazareth (4.16ff.); they recur in Jesus' reply to John the Baptist (Luke 7.22 = Matt.11.5): 'The poor have the good news preached to them', and above all in the Beatitudes (Luke 6.20ff.; cf. Polycarp 2.3):

> Blessed are you poor, for yours is the kingdom of God.
> Blessed are you that hunger now, for you shall be satisfied.
> Blessed are you that weep now, for you shall laugh.

Corresponding to the beatitudes on the poor, we find 'woes' on the rich and those who have plenty (6.24):

> But woe to you that are rich, for you have received your consolation.
> Woe to you that are full now, for you shall hunger.
> Woe to you that laugh now, for you shall mourn and weep.

The parable of the rich man and poor Lazarus is similar to this contrast of beatitudes on the poor and woes on the rich (Luke 16.19-31). The story of the rich farmer is no less critical (Luke 12.16-21).

> Fool! This night your soul is required of you; and the things you have prepared, whose will they be?

'The deceit of riches' is one of the thorns which choke the

growing seed of the Word and prevent it from bringing forth fruit (Mark 4.19).

The simile of the needle's eye is even more biting:

> It is easier for a camel to go through the eye of a needle than for a rich man to enter the kingdom of God (Mark 10.24 par.).

Only God's miracle can save him, 'for all things are possible with God' (Mark 10.27). It is significant that this uncompromising saying was modified in manuscripts at a very early stage. Also in this context belongs the fact that Jesus himself had no possessions: 'The Son of man has nowhere to lay his head' (Matt.8.20 = Luke 9.58), that he required those who were called to follow him not only to break with their families (Luke 9.59ff.; 14.26) but also to give up their possessions (Mark 1.16ff. par.; 10.17ff.,28ff. par.). When he sends the disciples out he requires extreme poverty of them (Luke 9.3; 10.4; cf. Mark 6.8f.); he also promises them that their renunciation of possessions will find recognition with God (Mark 10.28ff.). Jesus' polemic against concern for everyday needs (Matt.6.25-34) and his demand to renounce the use of force and legal proceedings, his requirement of unconditional generosity, go in the same direction:

> Give to every one who begs from you; and of him who takes away your goods, do not ask them again (Luke 6.30; cf. Barn.19.11; Did.1.5)

We can understand how at a later date the church father and ascetic Jerome, who was himself very critical of riches, could allow the objection to Jesus' demand in Matt.19.29 that 'it is difficult, harsh and contrary to nature' (*difficile est, durum est, et contra naturam*). He answers it by the Lord's saying in Matt.19.12: 'He who is able to receive this, let him receive it.'[2]

2 *Jesus' Free Attitude to Property*

However, this radical criticism of property and especially of riches is only one side of Jesus' ministry and preaching. We should note first that Jesus himself did not come from the proletariat of day-labourers and landless tenants, but from the middle class of Galilee, the skilled workers. Like his father, he was an artisan, a *tekton*, a Greek word which means mason, carpenter, cartwright and joiner all rolled into one (Mark 6.3). According to Justin Martyr he had 'made yokes and ploughs' (*Dial*.88.8). Two generations later, in the time of Domitian, two of his great-nephews are said to have worked a small piece of land (see below, pp.63f.). As far as we can tell, the disciples whom he called to follow him came from a similar social milieu. Zebedee, the father of James and John, employed day-labourers in his family business as well as his sons (Mark 1.20); another disciple, Levi, was summoned from the seat of custom (Mark 2.14f.) — the first evangelist identifies him with Matthew (Matt.9.9f.; 10.3). Even Jesus' conduct — unlike that of John the Baptist (Matt.11.18; Mark 1.6f.) — was not that of a rigorous ascetic.

Thus Jesus himself took for granted the owning of property in his immediate surroundings. He and his disciples were supported by the means of well-to-do women who followed him (Luke 8.2f.; cf. 10.38f.). In Capernaum he visits the house of his disciple Simon Peter and heals Peter's mother-in-law (Mark 1.29ff.). It is possible that this house served as a base for him during his preaching journeys. Excavations suggest that it perhaps became a house church at a later date; a Byzantine church was then erected on the site. Arguing against Pharisaic casuistry over sacrifice, Jesus enjoins that parents must be supported from their children's possessions, and refers back to the fourth commandment (Mark 7.9f.par.). In the same way, possessions are to be used to help those in need (Mark 12.41ff.; Matt.6.2; 25.40; Luke 10.30-37). In requiring money to be lent without hope of return (Matt.5.42 = Luke 6.30;6.34), Jesus presupposes property that can be lent. The chief publican Zacchaeus is ready to give half his possessions to the poor and to make amends fourfold to those who have been cheated: but he is not required to give up all his possessions (Luke 10.8f.). Jesus did not avoid contact with the rich and the privileged by any means; he was invited to banquets by them (Luke 7.36ff.; 11.37; 14.1,12; Mark 14.3ff.), and particularly by those with the worst reputation, the tax and excise farmers, who collaborated with the foreign occupying power (Mark 2.13-17). He was not an ascetic and was glad to join in festivals (John 2.1ff.); this made him incur the mockery of the pious:

> Behold, a glutton and a drunkard, a friend of tax-collectors and sinners (Matt.11.19 = Luke 7.34).

The one who is fond of celebrations and rejects fasting because it is out of place in the joy of the messianic feast (Mark 2.18ff.) does not look on property with the critical and fanatic eyes of the ascetic rigorist.

He held fellowship meals with his disciples, and for these, as the last supper shows, they relied on the support of well-to-do house-owners (Mark 14.14f.). Finally, it is striking that in his parables he often depicts the social milieu of Galilee with its great landowners, landlords, administrators and slaves, without engaging in any specifically social polemic (apart from the two parables mentioned above). Even servitude for debt and the use of slaves as entrepreneurs and bankers to increase the cash left with them (Matt.25.14ff. = Luke 19.12ff., cf. p.71 below) merely serve as a simile to portray God's demand. In the parable of the labourers in the vineyard those who had worked hard all day complain that they have been paid too little in comparison with those who came later and received the same wages. The employer answers with a classic definition of property which remains valid down to the present day:

> Am I not allowed to do what I choose with what belongs to me? (Matt.20.15)

In his parables Jesus evidently liked to single out unusual, vivid situations and typical situations of injustice; however, he did not use them for the 'social protest' which is so beloved today, but for a positive demonstration of God's will in respect of his coming kingdom.

3   *The Imminence of the Rule of God and the Love of the Father*

How are we to explain this contradiction? We should certainly not be in too much of a hurry to simplify it and rob it of its acuteness, say by explaining that property was legitimated by Jesus as something entrusted to men by the Creator, who required faithful stewardship of it. Jesus only fights against its misuse. This favourite interpretation of property as a 'loan' entrusted by God, which has played so great a role in modern Christian discussion of property, can certainly be found in the preaching of Jesus or of the early church (Luke 16.13; cf. 16.9, and I Cor.4.7f. in a metaphorical sense), but it is not of central significance. Nor is it a specifically Christian idea. It appears in the Old Testament and Judaism, and even among the Greeks. Thus in the fine verses of Euripides, we find:

> What is your profit? Profit but in name.
> Enough is quite sufficient for the wise.
> We are but stewards of the gifts of heaven.
> When gods desire, they take them back again.
> Possessions are not ours to call our own (*Phoen.*553ff.).

To understand Jesus' attitude to property we must return to his messianic preaching of the imminence of the kingdom of God which, in contrast to that of his forerunner, John the Baptist, no longer stands under the sign of judgment but under that of the all-victorious love of God. Because men experience forgiveness of their guilt, they themselves can forgive; because they receive the assurance that God's goodness supports and sustains their life, they must no longer fret about their everyday needs, but can pray like children, 'Give us this day our daily bread' (Luke 11.3 = Matt.6.11). Because they themselves have encountered the heavenly Father's boundless love, they must not relapse into anxiety about asserting themselves; they can even dare to love their enemies and can renounce the compulsion of using force in return (Matt.5.38-48; cf. Luke 6.27-36). Anyone who is dependent on his possessions and as a result forgets his neighbour lives in this state of anxious egoistic self-assertion:

he rejects God's commandment to love for the sake of the idol of mammon. God is near to the poor, the despised, the sick, as they stand before him with empty hands, like the prodigal son standing before his generous father. Jesus was not interested in any new theories about the rightness or wrongness of possessions in themselves, about the origin of property or its better distribution; rather he adopted the same scandalously free and untrammelled attitude to property as to the powers of the state, the alien Roman rule and its Jewish confederates. The imminence of the kingdom of God robs all these things of their power *de facto*, for in it 'many that are first will be last, and the last first' (Mark 10.31 = Matt.19.30; 20.16; Luke 13.30). Of course, Jesus attacks mammon with the utmost severity where it has captured men's hearts, because this gives it demonic character by which it blinds men's eyes to God's will — in concrete terms, to their neighbour's needs. Mammon is worshipped wherever men long for riches, are tied to riches, keep on increasing their possessions and want to dominate as a result of them. This radical criticism of riches may be rejected as hopeless enthusiasm, like the demand to renounce force and to love one's enemies, but particularly today, when there is so much talk of a 'definite utopia', one might well ask whether not only Christianity, but the whole of mankind does not need the goad which Jesus' message provides. Such different figures as Leo Tolstoi, Albert Schweitzer, Mahatma Gandhi, Toyohito Kagawa and Martin Luther King may be cited as examples.

The example of Jesus and his closest disciples shows that Jesus' message was also translated into action. Jesus required of his disciples that they should break with their families and renounce their own possessions, so that they could be like him in being completely prepared for serving the cause of the kingdom of God. His scandalous 'social' preaching was certainly one reason why he was condemned and executed by the Romans as a messianic pretender and rebel, though he did not follow the Zealots in demanding change in the system by force. Rather, the power that went out from him was much stronger than all human force.

4

The 'Love Communism' of the Primitive Community

The beginnings of the early community in Jerusalem after the appearances of the risen Jesus show that his message continued to have an effect.

I had already said that Luke has stylized his picture of the early community along the lines of popular philosophical terminology (see pp.8f. above). For example, the repetition of the formula 'they had all things in common' (*panta koina*) is reminiscent of the proverb coined by Aristotle (*Eth.Nic.* 1168b), 'the possession of friends is something held in common' (*koina ta philon*). Aristotle also introduces the term 'one soul', used by Luke in this context (4.32). However, it remains an open question whether primitive Christian sharing of goods, described by Ernst Troeltsch as 'love communism', is simply an idealistic invention of the author, as radical criticism assumes, or has some basis in history. 'Radical criticism' can refer to the fact that Luke makes apparently contradictory statements. At one point he talks about a complete sharing of goods (Acts 2.44; 4.32), but on the other hand it is reported that individuals like Barnabas and Ananias and Sapphira sold their land and brought the proceeds to the apostles. Of course, Ananias and Sapphira are said to have kept back half the proceeds and to have been punished promptly as a result (5.1-11).

It is striking that the atheistic philosopher Ernst Bloch had more confidence in the communism of the early community in Jerusalem than so-called radical criticism:

This community, built up on a communism of love, wants neither rich men nor poor men in a forced or ascetic sense. 'No one said that any of the things which he possessed was his own, but they had everything in common' (Acts 4.32). Their possessions were assembled from gifts, sufficient for the short interval which Jesus had still granted to the old earth. His saying about the lilies of the field and the birds of the air is by no means economically naive, but is deliberately enthusiastic. For if the steps of those who are to bury the world and its care are at the door, economic concern for the day after tomorrow is stupid.[1]

Here Ernst Bloch has a clearer view of the historical conditions than many so-called critical exegetes. This is the case at three points:

1. He bases the sharing of goods in the early community on the strong influence which the eschaton had on them: after the appearances of the risen Christ they expected him soon to come again as their Lord. This point recedes into the background in Luke, so it is easy to misunderstand his account.

2. Bloch stresses the spontaneous and voluntary character of this 'love communism'. It was not organized, nor was it subjected to external compulsion. The decisive thing was *koinonia*, not organization.

By contrast, the sharing of goods among the Essenes was strictly organized and fixed by law. It originally grew out of the protest against the unbounded quest of the Jewish aristocracy for wealth, during the Maccabean rebellion (1 QpHab.8.10ff.), and also had eschatological and utopian motives. Soon, however, it was given a firm legalistic structure. To some degree it became the law for the Jewish way of poverty (see above, p.19). According to the rule of Qumran, every novice who entered the order had to leave his possessions with the overseer. If after a year he was accepted, he had to make them over to the order (1 QS 1.11ff. and Josephus, *Bell*.2,122). All the needs of the members of the community were met from these resources and as a result of their own work in agriculture or crafts. In this way the order seems to have accumulated considerable riches. When Josephus says that the Essenes were 'despisers of riches', he is only talking of individual property. Common possessions were meant to make 'humiliating poverty' and 'inordinate riches' impossible. The rules were strict: anyone who made false statements about his possessions was excluded from the community for a year and had his rations cut by a quarter. The early community certainly did not have so well organized and forcible a 'sharing of goods'.

3. Bloch rightly refers back to the preaching of Jesus with its criticism of 'unrighteous mammon' and of anxiety. Jesus' message and his way of life were still remembered, and it would be quite incomprehensible if they did not continue to have some influence. Here the early church in Jerusalem was simply continuing Jesus' carefree attitude to the goods of this world. In view of the imminence of the coming Son of man, who was identical with Jesus, the barrier of possessions, which had done more than any other power to separate men down the millennia, had been brought down; anything which the individual had was freely put at the disposal of the community, as far as it was needed. The alleged contradiction between the two remarks in Luke, that 'no one said of his possessions that they belonged to him' and that individual landowners like the Levite Barnabas from Cyprus sold their land or houses and put the money at the disposal of the community, is only an apparent one. The mention of Barnabas does not point to a unique and special instance in Jerusalem. Barnabas was mentioned because he was known to the church in Antioch, by whom this piece of tradition was preserved. The church proudly pointed to him as an authority who had himself had a part in the 'love communism' of the Jerusalem church. This note (Acts 4.36) is presumably one of the references to Luke's Antiochene source. A charismatic-enthusiastic community was formed which assembled for daily worship; common meals were held (Acts 2.42); concern over possessions and the future retreated completely into the background; people lived from hand to mouth. The Lord was very near, and he had told people not to worry. The only real concern was missionary preaching among the Jews, including the Greek-speaking

diaspora Jews who had also settled in Jerusalem. The daily
needs of the community were met by selling the possessions
of those who had such resources; social distinctions were
virtually abolished, and there were no longer any poor in the
community (Acts 4.34). Yet others put their houses at the
disposal of the community as meeting places, like Mary, the
mother of John Mark (Acts 12.12). No one bothered with the
legal questions connected with property, with entries in land
registers or the like. The things of this age had become
inessential. Organization was kept to a minimum, and in view
of the intensive expectation of the return of Jesus, further
forward planning was completely absent. As a result, difficulties in distribution arose, especially as the community
grew quickly. Acts 6.1ff. reports how the 'widows' in the
Greek-speaking part of the community were neglected at the
daily distribution and how disputes arose as a result. In view
of the community's glowing expectation of an imminent end
and the enthusiasm brought about by the experience of the
spirit, people had no interest in economic production
organized on community lines, like that among the Essenes
of Qumran. The pressure from the Jewish environment and
the famine under Claudius during the forties (Acts II.28) also
contributed to the considerable economic distress suffered by
the community in Jerusalem. As a result the community in
Antioch – and probably other mission churches too – had to
leap to the rescue. The collections enjoined on Paul and
Barnabas at the Apostolic Council at Jerusalem about AD 48,
which the apostle was particularly concerned to achieve
among his mission communities, must also be understood
against this background. Twice he calls the original community in Jerusalem 'the poor' (Gal.2.10 and Rom.15.26).
On the one hand this is a religious title of honour, but at the
same time it indicates the economic distress in this community. The Jewish Christians in Palestine and Syria who had
separated from the mainstream church later called themselves
'Ebionites', in other words 'the poor'.

5

Paul and the Communities of the Gentile Christian Mission

1 The New Situation

In the Pauline mission communities and in the later development of primitive Christianity, we no longer come across the eschatological and enthusiastic form of sharing goods which we assume to have been practised by the earliest community in Jerusalem, on the basis of the reports in Acts. The reason for this is first, that the tension of the expectation of an imminent end was relaxed in favour of the task of world-wide mission, and secondly, that in the long run the form of 'love communism' practised in Jerusalem was just not possible. It was impossible to maintain a sharing of goods in a free form, without the kind of fixed organization and common production which we find, say, at Qumran. Further external compulsion was indispensable, and it was precisely this that was felt to be unacceptable. Free, charismatic community rather than a legalistic idea of order is typical of primitive Christianity. Even the Pauline communities did not have any clear organization or strict direction of the community. This only developed during the second century. The admonition of the apostle to the members of the community in Thessalonica that they are to earn their daily bread by manual labour, so that they do not cause any offence to outsiders and do not have to endure the lack of anything, shows that the problem of supporting themselves and owning possessions in conjunction with an enthusiastic expectation of the *parousia* still continued to concern at least some of those within the Pauline mission area (I Thess.4.12; 5.14). Presumably there were some who simply put their hands in

their pockets and let themselves be looked after by others. II
Thessalonians accentuates this admonition (3.7ff.), coming to
a climax in a maxim which was taken into the Soviet Russian
constitution: 'If any one will not work, let him not eat.'

At least in the genuine letters of Paul, the question of
poverty and riches, of possessions and lack of possessions, is
left entirely on one side. The term 'rich' (*plousios*) appears
only once in Paul, transferred to the pre-existent Christ, and
not therefore in a social context (II Cor.8.9), whereas in one
passage he refers the word 'poor' to himself ((II Cor.6.10). In
so doing he expresses the contradiction in his life as an
apostle:

> As poor, yet making many rich;
> as having nothing, and yet possessing everything.

Paul himself had no possessions. During his missionary
journeys he earned his keep by hard manual labour as a
tentmaker (Acts 18.3). He did not ask the communities to
look after him (I Cor.9), but accepted support offered freely
with gratitude (Phil. 2.25ff.; 4.15ff.). Accustomed to
extreme need, he was glad when he was sufficiently cared for
(Phil.4.11f.).

2   The Social Structure of the Gentile Christian Communities

The communities founded by Paul were certainly not
well-to-do. Thus he writes to the Christians in Corinth:

> For consider your call, brethren;
> not many of you were wise according to worldly stan-
> dards, not many were of noble birth (I Cor.1.26).

Of course this much-quoted remark should not be interpreted
in the wrong way. Paul says 'not many', not 'none at all'. We
cannot infer from this passage that the Pauline mission
communities were composed only of the proletariat and
slaves, nor may we make Paul an advocate of the Jewish way
of poverty. What Pliny the Younger, as governor of Bithynia
in Asia Minor, wrote to the emperor Trajan, also applied to
the communities founded during the mission of the apostle

to the Gentiles: 'many . . . of every class . . . are endangered now and will be endangered in the future' (by the new 'superstition': *multi enim . . . omnis ordinis . . . vocantur in periculum et vocabuntur*). That is, there were members of Christian communities in all strata of the populace, from slaves and freedmen to the local aristocracy, the decurions, and in some circumstances even to the nobility of the Senate. The old dispute whether the nephew of the emperor Domitian, Flavius Clemens and his wife, Flavia Domitilla, because of their Judaizing tendencies – thus Dio Cassius 67,14,1f. – or Flavius Clemens' niece of the same name, because of her conversion to Christianity – thus Eusebius, HE 3,18,4 – were executed or exiled by the emperor, has still not been settled. It shows that we must at least reckon with the possibility that in individual cases the new faith quickly penetrated to the heights of society. Evidence for this increases greatly in the second half of the second century (see below, pp.64f.).

The majority of early Christians will have belonged to the 'middle class' of antiquity from which the 'godfearers' of the Jewish mission were recruited (cf. Acts 13.43,50; 16.14; 17.4,17; 18.7). Women from the upper classes may also have been won over. It should also be noted that the Pauline mission was exclusively limited to the cities, and hardly reached country people. Even the lowest strata of ancient cities had a better social status than the uneducated and downtrodden tenants and peasants in the villages. For Pliny, it was a sign of the dangerous aggressiveness of the new sect that 'the contagion of that superstition has penetrated not the cities only, but the villages and the country' (*Ep.*10,96,9). But until the third century that was the exception. In the footsteps of Paul, the Christian faith, like all the missionary religions in antiquity, remained predominantly a city religion. Of course, Pliny's agitated report could be contrasted with the judgment of the rhetorician Aelius Aristides, written down about a generation later. Comparing the Christians with the Cynics, he stresses 'that they neither worship the gods, nor sit on city councils' (*Or.*46, II,404, ed. Dindorf); but this only says that because of the religious duties bound up with municipal offices they could not

undertake posts of this kind. This remains the case down to
the third century. The Pauline epistles and even more Luke's
Acts of the Apostles (see p.64 below) point to individual
Christians from the upper classes. In Corinth they included
Erastus, the city treasurer (Rom.16.23), Crispus, the ruler of
the synagogue (Acts 18.8), Stephanas and his household (I
Cor.1.16; 16.15,17), Prisca and Aquila, who evidently had a
business with branches and not only employed Paul in it but
also went bail for him (Acts 18.2,18,26; Rom.16.3); in
Colossae, Philemon, who not only had the slave Onesimus,
but also presided over a 'house church'; in Laodicea,
Nymphas (Philemon 2; Col.4.15). The list could be continued, and the role of well-to-do women should not be
overlooked. It was probably the rule that not only the 'father
of the house' but also the whole household dependent on
him, including the slaves, were baptized at the same time.
These names are mentioned because prominent Christians of
this kind and their households provided bases for mission. At
the same time, they stood out because on the whole they
were the relatively rare exceptions.

Paul himself says that the communities were predominantly poor and we have no reason for mistrusting him. Thus
he speaks of the 'extreme poverty' of the churches in
Macedonia (II Cor.8.2), which still did not prevent them
from devoting themselves with great self-sacrifice to the
decisive collection for the original community in Jerusalem.
Nevertheless, the scandals at the eucharist in Corinth (I
Cor.11.20ff.) show that at least at the beginning gross
differences could exist between the relatively well-to-do and
the poor. Individual members of the church evidently
confused it with a Dionysian festival and behaved accor-
dingly, whereas others 'went hungry'. Newly-converted
Hellenistic Gentile Christians from the Greek metropolis and
port first had to learn to take social responsibility for their
poorer fellow-members, since Hellenistic religions — which
were very strongly oriented on class lines — hardly knew
them. The lawyer Apuleius had to pay dearly in Corinth for
the mysteries of Isis and later incurred additional expense in
Rome at the mysteries of Osiris. He emerged from all this on
the verge of financial ruin (Apuleius, *Met.* 11,22,2; 23,1;

24,6; 28.1ff.) The missionary expansion of a new religion was not least suspect because of practices of this kind; similar insinuations were made about Paul (II Cor.2.17; 4.2; 11.13). This was probably one of the reasons why, in contrast to the Jerusalem missionaries, the apostle refused support from the communities and supported himself by his own manual labour (I Cor.9.6,13ff., see above, p.36). In his ethical admonitions he did not require complete abolition of differences in means, but looked for active and effective brotherly love (II Cor.8.13ff.). This means that the 'abundance' of some is to supply the 'want' of the brethren – e.g. in Jerusalem – 'that there may be equality (*isotes*)'. Similarly, in the paraenetic parts of his letters and elsewhere one can find the appeal to generosity and hospitality which was also already traditional in Judaism (Rom.12.13), for 'he who sows sparingly will also reap sparingly, and he who sows bountifully will also reap bountifully' (II Cor.9.6f.). The gifts of love not only supply the needs of the brethren, but also lead to grateful praise of God among those who receive them (II Cor.9.12). Conversely, in the so-called catalogue of vices he warns against avarice and cupidity (Rom.1.29; I Cor.5.10f.; 6.10; II Cor.9.5f.). The later epistle to the Colossians identifies these vices directly with idolatry (3.5).

3 The Eschatological Relativization of Property

Paul shares with Jesus and the first community in Jerusalem the view that the imminence of the *parousia* makes the possession of property a relative matter: 'The appointed time has grown very short' (I Cor.7.29). Even if the task of extending his mission to the ends of the then known world, as far as Spain, lies between the present and the *parousia*, the end is nevertheless near:

> The night is far gone, the day is at hand;
> Let us then cast off the works of darkness and put on the armour of light (Rom.13.12).

His summons to obedience to the state powers, which comes to a climax in his admonition to obedience (13.7), must also be seen in this eschatological perspective. Certainly, through

Christ all believers are freed and reconciled with God and
their neighbour. The limits set by nation, race, class
and — one may also add — property no longer stand. In the
community the believer has restored to him the lost image of
God, so that there is no longer

> Greek and Jew, circumcised and uncircumcised, barbarian,
> Scythian (the allegedly sub-human race in antiquity, see
> above p.5), slave, free man, but Christ is all and in all
> (Col.3.11; cf. Gal. 3.28).

The revolutionary force of statements like this, which
founded a new community in antiquity, can hardly be
measured. Boundaries were overcome here which hitherto
had been regarded as impassable throughout antiquity. But
precisely because in reality they are already free, slaves are
now not to seek to become freemen quickly, nor are Gentiles
to go over to Judaism and vice versa. Were they to do this,
they would be giving recognition to the old forces of this
world, which have been robbed of their power and whose end
is imminent. Paul admonishes the Corinthians: 'Do not
become slaves of men. So, brethren, in whatever state each
was called, there let him remain with God'(I Cor.7.23f.). This
also applies to the question of property:

> Further, that those . . . who buy be as though they had no
> goods, and those who deal with the world as though they
> had no dealings with it. For the form of this world is
> passing away (7.29ff.).

Here we have a revolution in the standard of values
previously taken for granted, the gaining of freedom on the
basis of a 'detachment' of the believer, motivated by the
nearness of the Lord and the end of the world. What is
accepted or takes place here and now is neither what
ultimately matters, nor is it the power that determines men.
Here we have to some degree Paul's equivalent to the
commandment 'Do not be anxious' in the preaching of Jesus
(cf. I Cor.7.32ff.; Matt.6.25ff. = Luke 12.22ff.). Paul
automatically follows the promise 'The Lord is at hand!' with
the admonition 'Do not be anxious' (Phil.4.5f.)

This freedom following from the 'detachment' achieved by

the believer continued when the imminent expectation of the *parousia* died down and people began to reckon with a — relatively — long duration of history. It gave the small 'sect' of Christians the strength to bear all the insults, oppression and persecution from the Roman state authorities which came during the first three centuries and to overcome them. Without any external force, but simply through the inner power of the words and actions of love, Christians succeeded in conquering the Roman empire.

Paul already found the basis for this detachment in the presence of salvation: 'For our citizenship is in heaven' (Phil.3.20). It will only be made manifest through the *parousia*: 'from where we await a saviour, the Lord Jesus Christ . . .' Colossians 3.3f is very similar: 'Your life is hid with Christ in God. When Christ who is our life appears, then you also will appear with him in glory.' In concrete terms, that means that concern for property and possessions had become a quite secondary matter. At the same time, it also means that the first Christians simply were not aware of the question which concerns us so much today: 'How can we make a better future for our threatened world?' They cannot give us a practicable programme of social ethics to solve the question of possessions, which has become so acute today as a result of industrialization. Not only is it that our world-wide industrial society, with all its technology, can only to a very limited degree be compared with the predominantly social structure of late antiquity; since the first Christians were a tiny minority, who were also politically suspect, they could not strive in their ethical action for the social reform of the Roman empire of the time. They had to limit themselves to the construction of a community ethics within an unfriendly, indeed hostile world, sustained by true love and humanity — but at the same time quite 'transitory' (I Cor.13.10). The best to be expected from the political authorities was tolerance, and this was only granted in AD 311; as a rule people believed that they would fall into the hands of anti-Christ, who would mount a last attack on the church and would then be vanquished at the *parousia* of Christ.

6

Attempts at Solving the Question of Property in the Community Ethics of Early Christianity

It follows from what has been said that the ethics of the early church was exclusively community ethics, binding on the community of believers. This is also the case with the question of property. Like the question of slavery, within the Christian community it seemed largely to have been solved. True, Paul sends the runaway slave Onesimus back to his Christian master Philemon, but he asks Philemon to accept the fugitive as a brother with equal rights. The requirement of the Didache, which was written in Syria at the beginning of the second century, is simple:

> Do not turn away the needy, but share everything with your brother, and do not say that it is your own (Did.4.8).

This attitude created a new structure within the Christian communities which is unique in antiquity. Travellers found a hospitable welcome (Heb.13.2; I Clem.10-12). Those who were capable of work had a right to work, and the disabled were adequately supported. The Christian 'philosopher' Aristides, who sent the first Apologia that we have to the emperor Hadrian about AD 125, sums up this new social attitude of the Christians in a few moving words:

> They walk in all humility and kindness, and falsehood is not found among them, and they love one another. They despise not the widow, and grieve not the orphan. He that hath distributeth liberally to him that hath not. If they see a stranger, they bring him under their roof, and rejoice over him, as it were their own brother: for they call

themselves brethren, not after the flesh, but after the spirit and in God; but when one of their poor passes away from the world, and any of them see him, then he provides for his burial according to his ability; and if they hear that any of their number is imprisoned or oppressed for the name of their Messiah, all of them provide for his needs, and if it is possible that he may be delivered, they deliver him. And if there is among them a man that is poor and needy, and they have not an abundance of necessaries, they fast two or three days that they may supply the needy with their necessary food.(15.7f.).

The Pseudo-Clementine romance cited above (p.1), puts forward what virtually amounts to a social programme for the community:

Give the unskilled an opportunity to earn their daily bread; give work to those who can do it, take care to look after those who are unable to work (*Ep.Clem.*8,6: GCS 42,12).

For Cyprian, the bishop and martyr in Carthage (died AD 258), it went without saying that the community should support at its own expense, in case of emergency, an actor who had given up his profession when he became a Christian and was also prohibited from teaching acting, bound up as it was with pagan mythology. There was, however, a significant qualification:

He must be content with frugal but innocent food. And let him not think that he is redeemed by an allowance to cease from sinning, since this is an advantage not to us, but to himself. What more he may wish he may seek thence, from such gain as takes men away from the banquet of Abraham, and Isaac, and Jacob, and leads them down, sadly and perniciously fattened in this world, to the eternal torments of hunger and thirst . . . If the church with you is not sufficient for this, to afford support for those in need, he may transfer himself to us (in Carthage), and here receive what may be necessary to him for food and clothing.[1]

By about AD 250, the Roman community was looking after about 1500 people in distress regularly, with only about 100 clergy. About eighty years earlier, Bishop Dionysius of Corinth had confirmed that this generosity of the Roman church was not limited to its own poor, but extended far beyond the boundaries of Rome:

> For this has been your custom from the beginning: to do good in divers ways to all the brethren, and to send supplies to many churches in every city: now relieving the poverty of the needy, now making provision, by the supplies which you have been sending from the beginning, for brethren in the mines (forced labour imposed by the state).[2]

Ignatius (about AD 116) is probably already alluding to this Roman custom when he describes the Roman community as 'leading in love' (*Rom.*, proem.) This tradition of many-sided and effective readiness to help among Roman Christians in the second and third centuries cannot simply be explained in terms of ecclesiastical or secular politics. Behind it stood a real solidarity of Christian faith. The lack of demands made by the clergy corresponds to this readiness to help. Thus while Origen can appeal to I Cor.9.14 and stress the right of the clergy to receive support, at the same time he adds that they should only ask for basic necessities, i.e. no more than the poor receive, so that the latter are not deprived of anything.[3]

In cases of catastrophe, readiness to help knew no bounds. When barbarian nomads laid waste Numidia in AD 253 and made many Christians homeless, Cyprian collected a spontaneous contribution of 100,000 sesterces for those who had been affected. This was from the relatively small community in Carthage — Cyprian claimed that he still knew all its members (*Ep.*62). We hear of similar generous help — even towards pagans — in epidemics of plague in Carthage, Alexandria and elsewhere.[4] This selfless, widespread care was all the more effective since from the second half of the second century the Roman empire was involved in an increasingly severe political and social crisis, which came to a climax in the middle of the third century. Even in the fourth century the emperor Julian the Apostate (361-363), an enemy of the Christians, told the pagan high priest Arsacius of Galatia 'that the godless Galileans feed not only their (poor) but ours also', whereas the pagan cult, in the revival of which the ruler was so interested, was a complete failure in the welfare of the poor (*Ep.* 84; p.430d, ed.Bidez). In this way the early Christian communities abolished complete penury among their own members and at the same time made a very good impression on outsiders, since such comprehensive care was alien to the pagan world.

However, real communism of goods no longer played a decisive part among the communities. As has already been said, it was hardly possible without some organized pressure. A radical demand for it was only made by outsiders, like the Gnostic Epiphanes, son of Carpocrates who founded the Carpocratians. He referred both to the philosophical doctrine of natural law and to Pauline freedom in his demand for complete equality of possessions:-

'The righteousness of God is a kind of fellowship on the basis of equality . . . For he makes no distinction between rich and poor.' On the other hand, the individual human laws contradict the divine command: 'As the laws could not punish human ignorance, they taught men to transgress the law (of God)', a thesis which the author bases on Rom.7.7 (Clem. Alex., *Strom*.III,6,1).

Faithful to ancient utopian pictures, he also argued for the sharing of wives: property becomes theft, exclusive possession of one wife becomes adultery. But this Gnostic Paulinism of an Alexandrian intellectual who is said to have died at the age of seventeen remained completely ineffectual. It was only of interest to fathers hostile to the Gnostics. Community of goods appeared on quite another basis among the Coenobitic monks of Egypt in the first half of the fourth century. Here the gospels' radical criticism of 'unrighteous mammon' comes to life again. Whether other influences — say the recollection of the Jewish sect of the Therapeutae, the Egyptian counterpart to the Essenes in Palestine — also play their part remains questionable. It is significant that such community was only possible because the individual subjected himself in

46   *Property and Riches in the Early Church*

complete obedience to the 'abbot' or to the monastery.

Christian communities may have attempted to solve the social 'problem' in their own sphere in a way unique in antiquity, but the question of the justice or injustice of property in excess of basic needs, i.e. of the possibility of reconciling riches with Christian life, remained an open question.

The answer to it was not a clear one, but took a variety of directions. We shall limit ourselves to three aspects: the radical criticism of property, the philosophical and ascetic motive of self-sufficiency and the compromise of effective compensation.

7

The Criticism of Property in Apocalyptic Christianity and its Tradition

1   The Influence of Crude Apocalyptic Polemic

These communities which continued the tradition of Palestinian Jewish Christianity, with its apocalyptic stamp, condemned riches in a form which was often quite crude. Thus the Epistle of James sharply attacks the way in which the rich and well-to-do have pride of place over the poor when the church is gathered together, for

> Has not God chosen those who are poor in the world to be rich in faith and heirs of the kingdom which he has promised to those who love him? . . . Is it not the rich who oppress you, is it not they who drag you into court? Is it not they who blaspheme that honourable name by which you are called? (James 2.1-7)

Similarly, the author utters a lament on the rich which is reminiscent of the polemic of the Jewish prophets and apocalyptic writers:

> Come now, you rich, weep and howl for the miseries that are coming upon you. Your riches have rotted and your garments are moth-eaten. Your gold and silver have rusted, and their rust will be evidence against you and will eat up your flesh like fire . . .
>
> Behold, the wages of the labourers who mowed your fields, which you kept back by fraud, cry out; and the cries of the harvesters have reached the ears of the Lord of hosts. You have lived on the earth in luxury and in pleasure; you have fattened your hearts in a day of

slaughter. You have condemned, you have killed the righteous man; he does not resist you (James 5.1-6).

These verses express equally both the oppression and also the revolt of the simple people in agricultural Palestine. It can be seen here that primitive Christianity was also a movement that was critical of society — even if it did not resort to revolutionary expedients, but delivered over the oppressors to God's judgment.

We find similar tones in the Revelation of John. Here the visionary exiled to Patmos 'on account of the word of God and the testimony of Jesus' (1.9) sees the final climax of the godlessness of the Roman empire in the rule of the anti-Christ, who persecutes the community mercilessly to the point of economic boycott (13.16f.). In glowing colours he depicts the fall of the whore of Babylon who is enthroned on the seven hills, i.e. the world city of Rome. At the same time its fall represents the end of inconceivable riches, and the writer's scorn for the consumption of luxuries can clearly be heard in his words:

And the merchants of the earth weep and mourn for her, since no one buys their cargo any more, cargo of gold, silver, jewels and pearls, fine linen, purple, silk and scarlet, all kinds of scented wood, all articles of ivory, all articles of costly wood, bronze, iron and marble, cinnamon, spice, incense, myrrh, frankincense, wine, oil, fine flour and wheat, cattle and sheep, horses and chariots, and slaves . . .

The merchants of these wares, who gained wealth from her, will stand far off, in fear of her torment, weeping and mourning aloud, 'Alas, alas, for the great city . . . in one hour all this wealth has been laid waste.'

God's judgment brings the annihilation of the luxurious civilization of this metropolis which dominated the whole world:

For thy merchants were the great men of the earth, and all nations were deceived by thy sorcery. And in her was found the blood of prophets and of saints, and of all who have been slain on earth (18.23f.).

Here the bitter rejection of riches and luxury is associated with crude opposition to the world power which wants to force Christians to acknowledge its pseudo-religious ruler-ideology through bloody persecution: 'A death sentence is pronounced on the world of Roman capitalism and its state.'[1] The aggressive, zealous undertone, the joy at the expected annihilation of the enemy, cannot of course be overlooked. At this point the popular hope of early Christianity was still closely bound up with the expectations of Jewish apocalyptic, which expressed its hope for the fall of 'godless rule' even in official Jewish prayers. There was also delight in depicting the torments of the godless and unmerciful rich in the apocalyptic accounts of hell (Apoc. Pet.30; Act.Thom.56; Sib.2,252ff.; cf. also already Luke 16.23ff.). The counterpart, the picture of the Christians' own hope, had quite realistic paradisal features. This can be seen from the Jewish-Christian Sibyllines, where apocalyptic themes are combined with the dream of the golden age (see pp.4f. above):

> And there are threefold springs of wine and milk and
>   honey.
> Earth the same for all, not divided by walls
> And fences, will then bear fruits more abundant
> Of its own accord; livelihood held in common, wealth
>   unapportioned.
> No pauper is there, no rich man, nor any tyrant,
> No slave, nor again any great, nor shall any be small,
> No kings, no rulers; but all share in common.[2]

Even the dream of 'freedom from rule' .is not a modern invention.

2 Thorough-going Criticism of Riches in the Community

Even within the community, however, immoderate possessions remained a stumbling block. In the apocalypse of Hermas (*Vis.*III 6,5-7), composed in Rome during the first half of the second century, the author compares the rich men in the community to round stones which are not suitable for building the church:

'When persecution comes, because of their wealth and

because of business they deny their Lord.' Hermas asks, 'Then when will they be useful for the building?' He is given the answer: 'When their wealth, which leads their soul astray, shall be cut off from them, then they will be useful to God. For just as the round stone cannot become spare, unless something be cut off and taken from it, so too they who have riches in this world cannot be useful to the Lord unless their wealth be cut away from them.'

Even the author, a small businessman living in Rome who perhaps also had some land to call his own, is regarded as 'rich'; his business separated him from God (*Vis*.II 3,1; cf. III 6,7). For 'riches make a man blind and blunt him towards the truth', even if they do not necessarily lead to his complete downfall (*Sim*.IX 30,4-31,2).

In the apocryphal writing *The Acts of Peter and the Twelve Apostles*, found at Nag Hammadi and only recently published,[3] Peter and the Twelve are sent out to heal the poor, but they are to have nothing at all to do with 'the rich of the city', who do not ask after Christ, 'but delight in their riches and their contempt for men'. For giving preference to the rich in the communities only brings about sin and transgression.[4]

Critical remarks of this kind can be multiplied at will, for example from the rigorist Tertullian, who could describe God as one who 'despises the rich and pleads the cause of the poor' (*Adv.Marc*.4,15). Christ, who himself was utterly poor, 'always justifies the poor and condemns the rich' (*De Patientia* 7,2f.). To the rich, luxury-loving matrons the churches seem small and contemptible: 'It is difficult to find a rich man in the house of God.' But even Tertullian cannot deny that they are there (*Ad Uxorem* 2,8,3, see pp.60f. below). The apologist Tertullian's Christian consciousness corresponds to his social criticism:

Whereas among pagan families, 'as a rule brotherliness ceases' when it is a question of family wealth, 'one in mind and soul, we do not hesitate to share our earthly goods with one another. All things are common among us but our wives.'[5]

However, the collections at worship described below (p.67)

show that even in Tertullian we may no longer presuppose a real 'sharing of goods'. The sharpness with which he attacks luxury and the search for pleasure and finery shows that these vices could already be found in the Christian community in Carthage about AD 200.

A little later the apologist Minucius Felix sounds almost like a Cynic philosopher in explaining why Christians despise riches:

> All of which things, if we do not lust after, we possess. Therefore, as he who treads a road is the happier the lighter he walks, so happier is he in this journey of life who lifts himself along in poverty, and does not breathe heavily under the burden of riches. And yet even if we thought wealth useful to us, we should ask it of God. Assuredly he might be able to indulge us in some measure, whose is the whole; but we would rather despise riches than possess them; we desire rather innocency, we rather entreat for patience, we prefer being good to being prodigal.[6]

3   The Motive of Asceticism

At this point the motive of asceticism comes very clearly to the fore in the rejection of riches; it is to gain increasing significance for the further development of the church. Eusebius reports that even one of the greatest theologians of the church, Origen, lived in extreme personal poverty (HE 6,3). There were wandering ascetics in Syria as early as the second century AD who had no possessions; we meet them in the Didache (11.5ff.). The ascetic stamp of the ideal of poverty to be found in the apocryphal Acts of Thomas, coming from the Syrian church at the beginning of the third century, is even more marked.

> Thomas, the twin brother of Jesus, 'eats only bread with salt, and his drink is water, and he wears (only) one garment . . . and takes. nothing from anyone, and what he has he gives to others'.[7] God has 'brought him into the poverty of the world, and invited him to true riches'. At God's command he becomes 'poor and needy and a stranger and a slave, despised and a prisoner and hungry

and thirsty and naked and weary'.[8] The theme of the radical *imitatio Christi* here is evident. For Christ himself deceived the demons 'by his form most unsightly and by his poverty and need'.[9] Thomas's preaching against covetousness, riches and gluttony is very much oriented on the preaching of Jesus, particularly the command not to be anxious. But at the same time it has a feature which does not occur in the message of Jesus. 'The wealth which is left here, and the possession which (comes) of the earth (and) grows old . . . support the body itself', that is, they bind men to transitory matter.[10] Thus sexual abstinence occupies the foreground of the apostle's preaching even more. In reality he does not require complete renunciation of property in principle,[11] but works of mercy.[12] Only the apostle himself is absolutely without possessions. In the newly-founded communities he institutes, among other things, social welfare for the poor, which is administered by deacons.[13] It is explicitly stressed 'that many believed him, and even some of the leading people'.[14] It is no coincidence that the official of highest rank to be converted, the commander Siphor, who put his house at the apostle's disposal, became presbyter and leader of a community.[15]

This remarkable work thus shows a division in the communities. The preachers, or a few 'perfect', who are practising the imitation of Christ, renounce possessions radically, whereas the community, which includes a number of well-to-do people, is summoned to have little regard for riches and to be generous towards the poor. By this they show that they no longer belong to the transitory material world, but to the invisible rule of Christ. Jesus' demand, understood in radical terms and interpreted dualistically, is no longer applied to all Christians, but transferred to individual ascetics, who have been singled out from the rest.

From the beginning of the third century we find a Christian monasticism in Egypt; the first actual monasteries, communities of monks, came into being a little later, not least under the influence of Pachomius. Here there were new possibilities of putting the renunciation of possessions and the sharing of goods into practice: in addition to the old ascetic ideal of a 'life like the angels', which follows Essene models (see p.9 above), there was also the social motive of helping the poor and the sick.[16] At almost the precise time when state and church were entering into an increasingly close alliance — probably out of some historical necessity, but not entirely for the good of Christianity — monasticism was creating a new form of life. Here the critical detachment from the world required by faith and particularly detachment from possessions could be realized in, and in some circumstances even over against, the 'imperial church' which was now coming into being. Without the new ascetic ideal of monasticism, the social-critical preaching of the great church fathers Basil, Gregory Nazianzen, John Chrysostom and Ambrose of Milan, with their stress on the obligations to the community of those with possessions, would hardly have been conceivable.

8

The Ideal of 'Self-sufficiency' in Popular Philosophy

1 Paul and the Influence of Popular Philosophy

The reference to asceticism introduces a further theme from the early Christian criticism of private property, namely, the demand for inner freedom. Paul was already putting forward this thesis:

> All things are lawful for me, but not all things are helpful. All things are lawful for me, but I will not be enslaved by anything(I Cor.6.12).

For this reason he stresses his self-sufficiency almost like an itinerant Cynic philosopher:

> I have learned, in whatever state I am, to be content. I know how to be abased, and I know how to abound; in any and all circumstances I have learned the secret of facing plenty and hunger, abundance and want (Phil.4.11f.)

In this stress on self-sufficiency (*autarkeia*, see above, p.9), we presumably have the combination of an ideal from Jewish wisdom with ideas from Greek popular philosophy. According to Pirke Aboth 4.1, Simeon ben Zoma (*c*.AD 100) gave the following definitions:

> Who is mighty? He who controls his disposition (*yezer*) ... Who is rich? He who rejoices in his portion; as it is said (Ps.128.2): 'When you eat of the labour of your hands, happy are you and it shall be well with you.' Rabbinic legend put these words into the mouth of the

elders of the South in their dialogue with Alexander the Great (*Tamid* 32a); it may be compared with the famous answer of the first cynic Diogenes to the same ruler's offer: 'Ask of me whatever you will.' 'Get out of my light' (Diog.Laert.6,38).

Yet there is an essential difference between Paul and the philosophical ideal. It was a pupil of Socrates, Antisthenes, the teacher of Diogenes, who was the first to formulate the maxim that 'the wise man is self-sufficient (*autarkes*)' (Diog.Laert.6,11). A later Cynic, Crates, is said to have followed in his footsteps. Using a formula for freeing slaves, he renounced his own possessions and gave them away.[1] This ascetic ideal of complete self-sufficiency was essentially derived from Socrates. Xenophon, the conservative, well-to-do country nobleman, praised his master because 'he was living on very little, and yet was wholly independent (*autarkestata*); he was strictly moderate (*enkratestaton*) in all his pleasures (*hedonai*)' (*Mem.*1,2,14). He also puts this confession on the lips of Socrates: 'My belief is that to have no wants is divine; to have as few as possible comes next to the divine' (1,6,10). A similar remark could come from one of the monastic fathers of the fourth century AD. The radical break with all possessions which is becoming visible here also served the philosopher guided by reason alone in his attempt to realize his autonomy. However, for Paul and early Christianity, to gain freedom was not an end in itself but a matter of gaining freedom to serve God's cause, to proclaim the gospel and to serve neighbours.

Of course, it is quite possible that the 'historical Socrates' came nearer to the Pauline 'freedom for service' than the philosophical ideal. In Plato's *Apology* he confesses that the God of Delphi had bidden him bring men to the insight that they are not wise: 'And by reason of this occupation I have no leisure to attend to any of the affairs of the state worth mentioning, or of my own, but am in vast poverty on account of my service to the god'(236/c).

Tatian, the Christian apologist and valiant ascetic, seems quite consistent in his standpoint when he abruptly challenges the pagan philosophers' claim to 'self-sufficiency':

'Who of your most eminent men has been free from vain boasting? Diogenes, who made such a parade of his independence with his tub, was seized with a bowel complaint through eating a raw polypus and lost his life by gluttony. Aristippus, walking about in a purple robe, led a profligate life, in accordance with his professed opinions. Plato, a philosopher, was sold by Dionysius for his gormandizing propensities' (*Or. ad Graec.* 2,1ff.). 'But do you, who have not the perception of these things, be instructed by us who know them; though you do profess to despise death, and to be sufficient of yourselves for everything. But this is a discipline in which philosophers are so greatly deficient, that some of them receive from the king of the Romans 600 aurei yearly, for no useful purpose they perform, but that they may not even wear a long beard without being paid for it'(19.1f.).

From the watch-tower of Tatian's rigorism, even the great Aristotle, 'who made happiness to consist in the things which give pleasure', and therefore consistently questions the felicity of those 'who have neither beauty, nor wealth, nor bodily strength, nor high birth', simply appears to be a fool: 'And these are the people who are supposed to do philosophy!' (2.5,9). He probably incorporated in his harmony of the gospels, the Diatessaron, an apocryphal saying of Jesus which was popular in the Syrian church: 'Accept nothing from anyone, and do not acquire anything in the world.'[2]

But the marriage with traditional philosophy could not be postponed, precisely in the sphere of ethics. The foundations for it had already been laid too long. A fine example of this is provided by the *Sentences of Sextus*, composed towards the end of the second century, the purpose of which was 'to bring the moral wisdom of the Greek sages under the wing of the church to whom all truth belongs'.[3] In them we find the lapidary admonition: 'Be content with a sufficiency' (*autarkeian askei*). Another saying gives the reason: 'The wise man without possessions is like God', for, 'God does not need anything, and the believer only needs God' (Sayings 98, 18, 49). The ideal of 'becoming like God' which appears here (fundamentally Socratic and Platonic) is matched by a wisdom-saying attributed to the Pythagoreans:

The man who is self-sufficient, without possessions, and wise, truly lives like God. He holds it to be the greatest riches not to require anything, not even for his natural needs. For in the acquisition of possessions, desire never rests. Rather, renunciation of injustice is enough for a good life.[4]

Here the idea of 'becoming like God' is connected with demands from the Sermon on the Mount (cf. Matt.5.48), like 'Give to him who begs from you' (5.42). On this, Sextus says:

Do not complain if someone robs you of your worldly goods. Hand over everything but freedom to the man who would rob you (Sayings 15,17).

2   Bourgeois Influence on the Ideal

The theme of self-sufficiency similarly appears in the deutero-Pauline Pastoral Epistles, which were written about the turn of the century, albeit in a rather different 'unascetic' form. It occurs in the context of controversy with Gnostic heresies, put forward by those who are 'bereft of the truth, imagining that godliness is a means of gain'.
The author then continues:

There is great gain in godliness with contentment (*autarkeian*); for we brought nothing into the world and we cannot take anything out of the world; but if we have food and clothing, with these we shall be content. But those who desire to be rich fall into temptation, into a snare, into many senseless and hurtful desires that plunge men into ruin and destruction (I Tim.6.6-9).

Here too the popular-philosophical background is obvious. However, freedom towards possessions, which is shown by contentment, does not so much serve a positive purpose, say the service of the gospel, as ward off harmful desires of the kind that are to be found among the Gnostic opponents of the author. Stoics and Cynics here would talk of 'passions'. But there is no ascetic rigorism. The individual is allowed possessions to a modest degree, necessary to support life.

This amounts to a deliberate rejection of radical asceticism and points to the entry of a bourgeois element into the early Christian community, a development which was historically inevitable. Although the word 'bourgeois' often has negative connotations nowadays, it should certainly not be taken in a derogatory sense. We might continue to ask today whether the 'bourgeois' phase of our history has not produced a far greater move towards learning tolerance and humanity, and has alleviated the tensions of class warfare. From the beginning, early Christianity was essentially a petty bourgeois movement. This was its strength. For in the historical form which it attained as a result, the Christian community found inner constancy, missionary strength and a sense of social responsibility which extended beyond its own ranks and courage to withstand state persecution. It is certainly no coincidence that in the Shepherd of Hermas, which in many ways is related to the Pastoral Epistles, the demand constantly recurs for Christians to be aliens in the world and to be content with 'a sufficient competence' (*autarkeia, Sim*.I,6 cf. *Mand*. VI,2,3). Riches, on the other hand, are given by God to be used in the service of the poor (*Sim*. I,6,8ff.). At the same time, this produces a fair exchange. The rich man, who is a poor man in God's eyes and whose prayer has no effect, supports the poor man with all that he has; in turn, the poor man prays for him:

> Therefore the two together complete the work . . . Blessed are they who are wealthy and understand that their riches are from the Lord, for he who understands this will also be able to do some good service (*Sim*.II,5-10).

These very simple remarks indicate the solution that the problems of poverty and riches was to find in the communities of the second century. It was a compromise. On the one hand, the traditional outright condemnation of the rich was maintained, but they were allowed a chance of salvation if they lived modestly and distributed their possessions generously to the poor. The solution which Clement of Alexandria — who had a much better philosophical and theological education — sought in his writing on 'The Rich Man's Salvation' was also along these lines. Clement, too, values *autarkeia* highly as a 'nurse of righteousness', since it is 'an attitude which is content with necessities and acquires by its own efforts those things which produce a happy life'.[5]

9

The Compromise of Effective Compensation

The way forward for the future was therefore neither a condemnation of possessions in principle (especially as the borderlines between poverty, a modest sufficiency and relative 'riches' were variable), nor the individualistic *autarkeia* of the wise man, but an attempt at constant, effective compensation. Anyone who did not want to involve himself in such a 'compromise with unrighteous mammon' always had the possibility of choosing the course of rigorous asceticism. Three viewpoints should be noted here.

1 The Positive Evaluation of Manual Labour and the Moderate Acquisition of Possessions

Recruits to early Christianity certainly did not come primarily from the lowest ranks of the proletariat of antiquity, without work and living on occasional earnings, nor from the slaves, who were restricted by law — it was not a slave religion. The early Christians were petty bourgeois: manual workers and craftsmen, small businessmen and workers on the land, all of whom had a great respect for honest labour (see pp.36ff. above). In his polemic, Celsus speaks contemptuously of 'wool-workers, shoemakers and clothmakers . . . quite uneducated and boorish men' who want to instruct others (*C.Cels*.3,55); this is the voice of the intellectual of antiquity, who despised manual labour. Even the rigorist Tertullian, who would most have liked to forbid all occupations which had even the slightest connection with pagan cults, asserts in his defence of Christianity:

We live among you, eating the same food, wearing the same attire, having the same habits, under the same necessities of existence. We are not Indian Brahmins or Gymnosophists, who dwell in woods and exile themselves from ordinary life. We do not forget the debt of gratitude we owe to God our Lord and Creator; we reject no creature of his hands, though certainly we exercise restraint upon ourselves, lest of any gift of his we make an immoderate or sinful use. So we live with you in the world, abjuring neither forum, nor shambles, nor bath, nor booth, nor workshop, nor inn, nor weekly market, nor any other places of commerce. We sail with you, and fight with you, and till the ground with you; and in like manner we unite with you in your business — even in the various arts we make public property of our works for your benefit (*Apol.* 43).

In his writing on idolatry he enumerates the occupations which he feels to be inappropriate for a Christian. He forbids Christians to be artists of any kind, engaged in making idols or building temples; magicians and astrologers, and also teachers and men of learning, since these communicate knowledge of pagan mythology in one form or another. Even the merchant who deals in the requisites of idolatry and at the same time hunts for deceitful gold, falls under suspicion (*De Idol.* 8-11). Here we can see something of that 'great refusal' which was typical of early Christianity. At the same time, however, the practical common-sense of the lawyer from Carthage also has its say. He deals with the objection that artists must earn a living in some way or another:

The plasterer knows both how to mend roofs, and lay on stuccos, and polish a cistern, and trace ogees, and draw in relief on party-walls many other ornaments beside likenesses. The painter too, and the marble mason, and the bronze worker, and every graver whatever, knows expansions of his own art, of course much easier of execution. For how much more easily does he who delineates a statue overlay a sideboard! How much sooner does he who carves a Mars out of a lime-tree fasten together a chest! . . There is only a difference in wages and rewards. But smaller

wages are compensated by more frequent earnings. How
many are the party walls which require statues? How many
the temples and shrines which are built for idols? But
houses, and official residences, and baths, and tenements,
how many are they? (*De idol*. 8,2-4; cf; *De Cult.Fem*. 1,6,1).

This means that the honest craftsman will still obtain the
remuneration he deserves, provided he has nothing to do with
idols and their temples. We find the same sober common sense
in Tertullian's advice to well-endowed daughters of the
Christian community to marry a poor fellow-Christian rather
than a pagan of the same social status. We find once again the
theme of compensation, which has already been noted:

> For if it is the poor, not the rich, whose are the kingdoms
> of the heavens, the rich will find more in the poor. She will
> be dowered with an ampler dowry from the goods of him
> who is rich in God. Let her be on an equality with him on
> earth, who in the heavens will perhaps not be so (*Ad
> Uxor*.2,8,4f.).

Even Tertullian knew how to adapt his teaching to the social
reality of the community. For all his forthright polemic
against riches, he too stresses that God also has the right 'to
grant riches', since 'with them many works of righteousness
and philanthropy can be achieved' (*Adv.Marc*.4,15,8).

This positive attitude towards respectable manual labour is
also to be found in an earlier period. Paul followed a good
rabbinic precedent in earning his living by manual work, and
enjoined the Thessalonians to work as energetically (see
pp.00 above). Even when attention was exclusively focused
on the coming kingdom of God, it was impossible to avoid
the 'pressure of work' which is now indissolubly bound up
with human existence (Gen.3.17ff.). Idlers were therefore
given short shrift by the communities. The Didache is
generally well-disposed towards the poor, but it advises that
while anyone who comes 'in the name of the Lord' is to be
received as a guest, he must also be carefully investigated.
Presumably there have been some unfortunate experiences.

> If he who comes is a traveller, help him as much as you
> can, but he shall not remain with you more than two days,

or, if need be, three. And if he wishes to settle among you and has a craft, let him work for his bread. But if he has no craft, provide for him according to your understanding, so that no man shall live among you in idleness because he is a Christian. But if he will not do so, he is making traffic of Christ; beware of such! (Did.12).

The satirist Lucian of Samosata has a long account of the way in which the Christians of Syria allowed themselves to be taken in and exploited by Peregrinus Proteus, a travelling philosopher and good-for-nothing, who gave himself out to be a Christian teacher and believer:

So if any charlatan and trickster, able to profit by occasions, comes among them, he quickly acquires sudden wealth by imposing upon simple folk.[1]

Certainly this is a caricature and an exaggeration, but Lucian is nevertheless indicating an acute problem among the Syrian communities, and probably not only there. This is clear from the Didache's mistrust of travelling prophets who allow the community to look after them. The *Didascalia apostolorum* follows in its footsteps:

Do you the faithful, therefore, all of you, daily and hourly, whenever you are not in the church, devote yourselves to your work; so that in all the conduct of your life you may either be occupied in the things of the Lord or engaged upon your work, and may never be idle . . .
Therefore, be always working, for idleness is a blot for which there is no cure. But if any man among you will not work, let him not eat; for the Lord God also hates sluggards: for it is not possible for a sluggard to be a believer.[2]

Industrious and frugal people, who also supported each other, in time acquired modest possessions, whether they deliberately sought them or not. Hegesippus tells how two great-nephews of Jesus administered a small estate of 39 plethra which was rated for tax at 9000 denarii. When they were brought before the emperor Domitian because of their Davidic descent,

They showed him their hands and the hardness of their skin and the calluses on their hands which came from hard work, to show that they were manual workers.

Despising them as 'common people', the emperor sent them home, where they were held in great respect as 'confessors' (Eusebius, HE 4.20). The Epistle to the Hebrews, which also comes from the time of Domitian, shows that the Christians in the community to which the letter is sent – probably in Rome – not only 'serve the saints (probably the communities in Palestine)' (6.20), but also 'joyfully accepted the plundering of your property (by the state)' (10.34). So they cannot have been completely without means.

2   The Increase in Members from the Upper Strata in the Communities

In time, more and more members of the upper classes came into contact with the church, and Christians neither could nor wanted to exclude them. We can already see how ambiguous the situation was from Luke. On the one hand, his gospel sets out an explicit 'theology of the poor', so that in the interpretation of the parable in 14.33, which is probably redactional, he can make Jesus say: 'Whoever of you does not renounce all that he has cannot be my disciple.' Nevertheless, he did not feel it a contradiction that he should dedicate his two-volume work to the well-born (*kratistos* = *egregius*, 1.3) Theophilus and take a special pleasure in enumerating prominent people who joined Jesus and his community. The list of such people extends from Joanna the wife of Chusa, one of the financial administrators of Herod Antipas, through the centurion Cornelius; the Athenian assessor, Dionysius; Menahem, the boyhood friend of Herod Antipas and so on, to Sergius Paulus, governor of Cyprus. A particular source of upper-class members for the early church was the group of godfearers on whom the Gentile-Christian mission concentrated its attention (see above, p.37); perhaps Luke himself came from this milieu. This development, the penetration of the Christian message into the ranks of the upper classes, which is already indicated – with a certain degree of pride – by the *auctor ad Theophilum*, continued in the second century, even if the overwhelming majority of Christians came from the simple people. According to Eusebius (HE 5,21,1), in the time of Commodus (180-192),

> Large numbers even of those at Rome, highly distinguished for wealth and birth, were advancing towards their own salvation with all their households and kindred.

Even the emperor's mistress, Marcia, came close to Christianity. She received Victor, bishop of Rome, and brought about the release of Christians condemned to forced labour in the quarries of Sardinia (see below, p.71). At about the same time the client king Abgar IX of Adiabene (AD 174-214) on the Parthian border was converted to Christianity. The strongly ascetic Acts of Thomas (pp.51f. above) probably reflects these events. Here kings, members of royal families, high officials and – not least – well-to-do women are converted to Christianity. At the same time we hear from Tertullian that Gentiles of 'every status' (*omnem dignitatem; Ad Nat.*1,1,2; *Apol.*1,7) come over to Christianity (see above, pp.36f.). Indeed Christians even enter the ranks of the senators (*Apol.*37,4; cf. *Ad Scap.*4,5f.). This development, once begun, could not be stopped. The mission had either to address all classes, or it had to close its ranks and become an ascetic sect, hostile to the world, or even a revolutionary movement. The decision in favour of social universalism had, in fact, already been taken by Paul. It is striking that the pagan opponents of Christianity, from Celsus to Julian, nevertheless regarded it as a subversive and hostile sect, although the course of negative regression had in fact been ruled out.

3   Comprehensive Care of the Poor and its Basis

We have already referred to the care for the poor in the early Christian communities, which was unique in antiquity. By this means an attempt was made to achieve a relative balance between rich and poor (see above, pp.42ff.). This meant that the communities had to have considerable means at their disposal. These came from free gifts which were collected at services, or even from particular settlements. This custom

already began among the Pauline communities and can be
traced onwards from there. Such intensive care of the poor
and charitable activity did, however, presuppose that the
majority of members of the community had a regular
income. This is how we are to understand the admonition
which appears in the instruction to newly-converted Christians contained in the Epistle to the Ephesians, a work which
probably comes from one of Paul's pupils (4.28; cf.Act.
Thom.58):

> Let the thief no longer steal, but rather let him labour,
> doing honest work with his hands, so that he may be able
> to give to those in need.

Only those who are themselves earning can be prepared to
offer help to others. What is said of the former thief of
course also applies to the rich. They are not to set their hope
proudly on uncertain riches,

> but on God who richly furnishes us with everything to
> enjoy. They are to do good, to be rich in good deeds,
> liberal and generous, thus laying up for themselves a good
> foundation for the future, so that they may take hold of
> the life which is life indeed (I Tim.6.17ff.).

Elsewhere the verdict on riches is strict (see above, pp.47ff.),
but here it is relatively mild; the rich have a chance of good
works; the idea of merit which derives from the Jewish
tradition is not to be left out of account. The argument of I
Clement goes in a similar direction, also introducing the
theme of the unity of the body of Christ:

> Let, therefore, our whole body (the church) be preserved
> in Christ Jesus, and let each be subject to his neighbour,
> according to the position granted to him. Let the strong
> care for the weak and let the weak reverence the strong.(!)
> Let the rich man bestow help on the poor and let the poor
> give thanks to God, that he gave him one to supply his
> needs . . . (38.1f.).

The proximity of the ideas here to those of Jewish wisdom
teaching, which had a strong influence on the practice of the
early Christian communities, is unmistakable in all three

passages. The way to the mutual exchange between poor and rich that we found in Hermas has ceased to be a long one (see p.58 above). While we may have theological hesitations about statements of this kind, in view of the situation of the community at the beginning of the second century they were practical and effective.

Paul could already put forward a similar argument over the collection for the 'poor' in Jerusalem:

> He who sows sparingly will also reap sparingly, and he who sows bountifully will also reap bountifully . . . for God loves a cheerful giver (II Cor.9.6f.).

He gives the very practical instruction that each Christian in Corinth should put something aside on the first day of the week, i.e. on Sunday (I Cor.16.2). Both Justin (*c*.150) and Tertullian (*c*.200) give a similar picture of the custom of the communities in Rome and Carthage at their services:

> And those who are well to do, and willing, give what each thinks fit, and what is collected is deposited with the president, who succours the orphans and widows, and those who through sickness or any other cause are in want, and those who are in bonds, and the strangers among us, and in a word takes care of all who are in need (Justin, *Apol*.67,6).

> Though we have our treasure-chest, it is not made up of purchase money, as of a religion that has its price. On the monthly collection day, if he likes, each puts in a small donation; but only if it be his pleasure, and only if he be able: for there is no compulsion; all is voluntary. These gifts are, as it were, piety's deposit fund. For they are not taken thence and spent on feasts, and drinking-bouts, and eating-houses, but to support and bury poor people, to supply the wants of boys and girls destitute of means and parents, and of old persons confined now to the house; such, too, as have suffered shipwreck; and if there happen to be any in the mines, or banished to the islands, or shut up in the prisons, for nothing but their fidelity to the cause of God's church, they become the nurslings of their confession. But it is mainly the deeds of a love so noble that lead many to put a brand upon us. See, they say, how

they love one another, for themselves are animated by mutual hatred; how they are ready even to die for one another, for they themselves will sooner put to death (Tertullian, *Apol.* 39, 5-7).

Another contributory factor to this readiness for sacrifice was the idea, common in antiquity, that God is the owner and giver of all good gifts (cf. James 1.17). Thus generosity could be interpreted as an 'imitation of God'; for God gives everyone what is necessary out of his inexhaustible riches, because of his 'benevolence to men' (*philanthropia*) (see above, pp.1f.). When there are anxious complaints about his regulations for eating, Paul quotes a saying from the Psalms which could also be applied to all other goods: 'The earth is the Lord's and the fullness thereof' (I Cor.10.26 = Ps.24.1). There is a similar thought in Hermas, that in the last resort all riches are ultimately the possession and the gift of God (see p.58 above). This theme constantly recurs in the later fathers, whether they are recalling the 'primal communism' of paradise when all had everything in common, or whether they derive from it the idea that possessions are a 'loan' made to man by God for which he will demand a reckoning (see p.29 above). The latter notion is much more common. A late collection made by John of Damascus contains a quotation from an apocryphal 'Teaching of Peter', which is typical of this early Christian verdict on riches:

Rich is that man who has compassion on many and who in imitation of God gives of what he has. For God has given to all all of that which he has made. Understand then (ye) rich men that ye must serve since ye have received more than ye yourselves need. Learn that others lack what ye have in abundance. Be ashamed to retain other people's property. Imitate God's equity, and no one will be poor.[3]

God's goodness enlists the believer in its service and compels him to ward off poverty with the aid of his possessions. The rich man is the one who can give richly (cf. already Mark 12.41ff. = Luke 21.1ff.). From this there automatically follows the principle that the man with possessions who closes his heart and his hand to those in need shuts himself off from the love of God and thus from salvation:

But if any one has the world's goods and sees his brother in need, yet closes his heart against him, how does God's love abide in him? (I John 3.17)

Modern commentators are fond of quoting Mandaean parallels to this well-known saying from I John. In reality, however, we have here a basic theme of early Christian ethics which has its roots in Judaism, though its real point comes through its application to the love of God in the person and work of Christ (John 3.16; 17.26; I John 4.7ff.). In the end, the appeal to God as the giver of all good gifts and the theme of the 'imitation of God' in early Christianity must be seen from the perspective of christology.

4   Three Examples from the Roman Community

For the communities of the second and third centuries with their often well-organized, generous care for the poor and social concern, which called for a constant stream of money and responsible administration of it, this 'compromise', which did not reject the rich but laid extra financial demands on them, was the only practicable expedient. As a result, possessions acquired a contradictory aspect. They were regarded simultaneously as a dangerous threat and a supreme obligation. This tension could only be removed by specific action. Suspicion of riches largely continued in the communities, but abundant giving was nevertheless sought and appreciation of it also reflected in part on the giver.

Here are three instances, which all come from the Roman community, as we are best informed about it in the second and at the beginning of the third century:

1. Marcion, son of the Bishop of Sinope, a well-to-do shipowner from Asia Minor, gave the considerable sum of 200,000 sesterces on entering the Roman community (c.AD 139). It is uncertain whether this was all his wealth, or only part of it. One thing is certain, that he earned his fortune as a Christian, despite his ascetic tendencies (though of course he had been excommunicated in the East before his arrival in Rome). Five years later, when he was expelled from the Roman community, this great sum was immediately returned

to him.[4] The community therefore seems constantly to have had considerable liquid means at its disposal.

2. The apocryphal acts of the apostles also reflect this changed attitude towards members of the upper classes and their riches. Their primitively didactic, romance-like narratives, interspersed with crude miracles, correspond to the expectations of the simple members of the community. It would be possible to construct something like an 'ideal' social history of Christianity on the basis of them.

The earliest acts of Peter, composed towards the end of the second century, are particularly fond of telling of the conversion of rich and well-to-do people. The matron Eubula is helped by Peter in a miraculous way to regain money stolen from her by Simon Magus. When she becomes a believer, 'having recovered all her property, she gave it for the care of the poor'.[5] The Roman senator Marcellus, who is led astray by Simon and rescued by Peter, gives over his house to widows and Christian virgins: 'For the things that are called mine, to whom do they belong but you?'[6] As the result of a vision, the rich Chryse, who 'since her birth has never used a silver or glass vessel, but only golden ones', bestows 10,000 gold denarii on Peter. He accepts these, despite the objection that 'she is notorious all over Rome for fornication'. The apostle confidently replies: 'She was bringing it as a debtor to Christ, and is giving it to Christ's servants; for he himself has provided for them.'[7] The story of the woman who was a sinner in Luke 7.36-50 may have served as a model here, but at the same time it is possible to see an indication that there was not too much narrow-mindedness over the acceptance of gifts in view of the great social tasks of the community. According to Harnack's calculations the Roman church had to provide between 500,000 and 1,000,000 sesterces a year in the middle of the third century for the support of the 1500 needy people who have already been mentioned.[8] Such a financial burden could only be supported if there was a regular financial influx into the community and an administration which functioned well.

3. The third example gives us a glimpse of the development

of this administration and the human problems involved in it. The evidence adduced so far is predominantly of an idealistic literary character, with little specific biographical detail; the foreground is often occupied by the ideal demand or the apologetic description rather than human reality and its conflicts. Hippolytus' *Refutation of all Heresies*, rediscovered in 1842, contains a brief biography of Hippolytus' opponent and counter-bishop, Callistus of Rome. It is, of course, polemical and is extremely distorted. Here we have a view of the chequered personal fate of a bishop of the Roman church, whose work was also dominated by social problems (*Ref. Her.* 9,12). H. Gülzow has recently clarified the historical and sociological background of this *Vita* in exemplary fashion.[9] Callistus was originally a slave of the Christian imperial 'official' Carpophorus, who was himself either a slave or a freedman, but nevertheless enjoyed considerable respect because of his position. Callistus, who probably grew up as a Christian, was involved by his master Carpophorus in some rather risky banking on his own account. 'As time passed, not a few deposits were entrusted to him by widows and brethren thanks to the reputation of Carpophorus'(12,1). However, possibly because of constant devaluation, his banking ran into difficulties and he attempted to abscond. The attempt misfired, and his master put him in a slaves' prison. He was released from it through the pleas of his fellow Christians. Carpophorus' unscrupulous self-interest and his obligations as a Christian were clearly in conflict here. Released from prison, Callistus, seeking to call in some of the debts outstanding to him, rushed into the synagogue on a sabbath, hoping to meet some of those who owed him money. A tumult arose, the Jews dragged him before the prefect of the city, Fuscian, and charged him with disturbing their worship and being a Christian.

Fuscian had him scourged and deported to the lead mines in Sardinia (AD 188), where a considerable number of Christians were already working as state slaves. A little later bishop Victor, with the help of Marcia, the concubine of the emperor Commodus, managed to achieve the release of the Christian prisoners in Sardinia (see p.65 above); an imperial eunuch and Christian priest Hyacinthus brought the letter of emancipation to the governor of Sardinia. Callistus was among those freed; as a 'confessor' who had been deported for his faith he was accepted into the clergy. His former master no longer had any claim on the freeman. Possibly to avoid conflicts, bishop Victor sent Callistus to live in Antium and paid him a monthly allowance for food. We may also see in this treatment of the former slave a tendency to mistrust his earlier master. Victor's successor in the bishopric, Zephyrinus, made Callistus his closest 'collaborator in organizing the clergy' and 'assigned him the supervision of the *coemeterium*' (12,14). In other words, Callistus was entrusted with the supervision of the burial places of the Roman community. Anxiety about an honourable burial was a special problem to simple people in antiquity, including slaves, and led to numerous burial clubs. As the evidence of Aristides shows (see p.43 above), this area was also included in Christian social welfare from the beginning, following Jewish tradition. The first burial places of the Roman church depended on gifts of money made by rich Christians; the former slave Callistus seems to have done sterling work in this area, by making the support of the cemeteries the immediate task of the communities.

If the archaeologists are right in unanimously putting the development of the cemeteries in the time between Caracalla (211-217) and Severus Alexander (222-235), then the success of Callistus, who was responsible for the cemeteries for twenty years during this period, is obvious.[10]

The former slave now occupied the most influential office at the bishop's disposal: the entire administration of community finances, including care for the poor, was in his hands. The community were so satisfied with his performance of this difficult task that after the death of Zephyrinus in AD 217 he was elected bishop, despite his lowly origin. The well-to-do and theologically well-educated Hippolytus, who had the best of connections with the imperial household, went away empty and was chosen as counter-bishop by a minority. The community of 'intellectuals' who gathered round him soon sank to the level of a school. The man from the ordinary people, the former slave who effectively represented the interests of broad areas of the community, seemed to be more trustworthy. He proved his good sense not only in rejecting rigorism in the question of repentance, but also in allowing the unions of well-to-do Christian women with Christian slaves or freedmen to be fully valid marriages — against traditional Roman legal thinking. In this way he solved an ethical emergency (Hippolytus, *Ref.Her.*9,12,24). According to Gülzow, this is the 'first clear acknowledgment after the New Testament period of the equal rights of slaves, outside worship and the arena'.[11]

10

Clement of Alexandria: The Rich Man's Salvation

The development sketched out so far was also written down in theological form. Clement of Alexandria (died before 215) wrote a treatise on the theme with which we are concerned, the title of which, *The Rich Man's Salvation* has already been mentioned. This writing simply sets out to give a theological foundation to the compromise which had already been put into practice, but still involved a good deal of tension. Drawing abundantly on his philosophical learning, Clement sets out his thought in the form of a sermon on the rich man and Jesus (Mark 10.17-31). He rejects the literal interpretation put forward by radical asceticism and seeks to 'internalize' Jesus' demand. The heart must be cleansed of its desire for riches. Voluntary poverty is not yet completely identical with the freedom of man's disposition from damaging passions, which is what Jesus requires. The Stoic influence is unmistakable: 'He who casts away worldly wealth can still be rich in the passions . . . We must therefore renounce those possessions that are injurious, not those that are capable of being serviceable, if one knows the right use of them'(15,2,4). This means two things: first, riches are not evil 'in themselves'. They are neutral, an 'intermediate matter'. Everything depends on the right use of them. This is a good Stoic way of putting things. Secondly, the rich man is not excluded from the kingdom of heaven for being rich, but as a sinner who refuses repentance. Extreme need 'bends the thought' and keeps it from divine things (12,5; cf.18,5); moderate means not only drive away care but also offer the possibility of doing works of love (13,1). The positive side of possessions is also noted here: used moderately and responsibly, they can also give a man freedom, though this freedom must always, of course, include the freedom of his neighbour. Thus possessions, rightly understood, are an instrument given by God (14,1ff.), indeed they are God's gift, which we receive for our brother's sake and not for our own (16,3). Everything depends on using riches to supply the need of one's fellow-men:

> For he who holds possessions . . . and houses, as the gifts of God; and ministers from them to the God who gives them for the salvation of men; and knows that he possesses them more for the sake of the brethren than his own; and is superior to the possession of them, not the slave of the things he possesses; and does not carry them about in his soul, nor bind and circumscribe his life with them, but is ever labouring at some good and divine work, even should he be necessarily some time or other deprived of them, is able with cheerful mind to bear their removal equally with their abundance. This is he who is blessed by the Lord, and called poor in spirit, a meet heir of the kingdom of heaven, not one who could not live rich (16.3).

The only unjust thing is to be greedy in seeking possessions for one's own sole use. As in I Tim. and in Hermas, the motive of exchange appears: 'By giving the perishing things of the world, he receives in exchange for these an eternal mansion in the heavens'(32.1).

For all Clement's concern to find a 'liberal' way between radical asceticism and a clear-cut justification of riches, compared with the preaching of Jesus his solution remains unsatisfactory, because in part it twists the gospel sayings. On the other hand, a positive evaluation must be made: he stresses energetically the absolute religious and social obligations which go with property. Property is the gift of God and in all cases is there to meet the needs of others.

Thus this short, sermon-like writing marks a revolution in the spiritual and sociological situation of the church. At that time Alexandria was not only the largest city of the Greek-speaking East, but at the same time also the richest in the whole empire, the trade centre for India, the Orient and the Mediterranean, a city which had both a unique educational tradition and a luxurious style of life second to none. A spurious letter of Hadrian's, though only coming from the fourth century, gives a satirical description of it:

> The city is well-to-do, rich, luxurious; no one in it is inactive. Some are glass-blowers, others make paper, yet others weave linen; all are engaged in some work or other . . . The only God they have is money (*unus illis deus nummus est*); this deity is worshipped by Christians, Jews and pagans alike.[1]

Leaving aside the last sentence, which is part of the anti-Christian polemic of the post-Constantine period, the description also fits the earlier period. Evidently Clement was seeking a hearing among educated and well-to-do groups in his writing on the rich young man. He also addresses them in his larger work 'The Teacher' (*Paedagogus*). In Books 2 and 3 he attacks the unbridled luxury of the upper classes of Alexandrian society with inexorable sharpness. For example, at the end of Book 2 he attacks the desire of prominent women to adorn themselves with gold and precious stones. Evidently there were about 200 of these Christian matrons in Alexandria, whose argument was as follows:

> 'Why may I not use what God has made? I have it by me, why may I not enjoy it? For whom were these things made, then, if not for us?'

According to Clement, people who talk like this do not know God's will:

> For first necessaries, such as water and air, he supplies free to all; and what is not necessary, he has hid in the earth and water . . . Behold, the whole heaven is lighted up and you do not seek God; but gold which is hidden, and jewels, are dug up by those among us who are condemned to death.

This argument from natural law is followed by Clement's own theological observations, which indeed form the beginning of a Christian argument:

But if all things have been conferred on you, and all things allowed you, and 'if all things are lawful, yet all things are not expedient', says the apostle (I Cor.10.23). God brought our race into communion by first imparting what was his own, when he gave his own word, common to all, and made all things for all (John 1.1ff.). All things therefore are common, and not for the rich to appropriate an undue share. That expression, therefore, 'I possess, and possess in abundance: why then should I not enjoy?', is suitable neither to the man, nor to society. But more worthy of love is that: 'I have: why should I not give to those who need?' For this is the true luxury – the treasured wealth. But that which is squandered on foolish lusts is to be reckoned waste, not expenditure. For God has given us . . . the liberty of use, but only so far as necessary; and he has determined that the use should be common. And it is monstrous for one to live in luxury, while many are in want.[2]

Thus Clement counters the extravagance of the well-to-do neither with the threat of the horrors of Jewish-Christian apocalyptic nor with the rigorous ascetic ideal of the later Egyptian monks, but with reasonable, disciplined moderation, which is guided by the 'Logos' (the 'Word' of John 1.1) and gives a full share to the neighbour in need. The aim of this instruction by the Logos is not a flight from the world, but a reasonable, moderate and at the same time generous use of worldly goods. Steadfast mastery of self leads to inner detachment from them. Riches are like a serpent which administers a fatal bite to those who are inexperienced, 'unless one, despising them, use them skilfully, so as to crush the creature by the charm of the Word, and himself escape unscathed' (*Paed*.3,35,1). Of course, anyone who has such mastery over his desires by virtue of the Logos knows that in reality 'only those (i.e. the Christians) are rich'; independently of their external situation they dispose of 'the best possession to its possessor, rendering man truly blessed' (3,36,1,12).

Thus in Clement traditions of Jewish wisdom, Stoic ethics and the message of the New Testament combine with the specific situation of the Alexandrian church in a new synthesis which is to point the way forward for the later church. The generally expressed radical and rigorist criticism of property was toned down and made more inward, though the possibility of completely renouncing possessions remained open. Riches were judged critically, but were no longer ruled out in principle; stress was laid, rather, on strict obligations to the community and the right use of them. Inner freedom in the detachment of faith had to prove itself in generosity and the renunciation of avarice and luxury.

11

Cyprian of Carthage: On Good Works and Almsgiving

For a Western counterpart to Clement's writing, coming from the Latin-speaking church, one might turn to the treatise of Cyprian, Bishop of Carthage, *On Good Works and Almsgiving*. It was written about fifty or sixty years later, between 253 and 256. Cyprian came from a prominent family, presumably part of the nobility of the city. According to the account of his biographer, Pontius, even while he was a catechumen he 'sold his property and distributed almost all the proceedings to provide sustenance for countless people who were in need' (*Vita* 2). That is, he seems to have distributed his personal possessions and made over his estates to the church. When persecution became imminent, however, he took back the estates as private or family property, to prevent their being requisitioned by the imperial authorities.[1] This rigorously ascetic, but also sovereign attitude is typical of the author of the brief work in which — in contrast to that of Clement of Alexandria — philosophical features fade into the background in the face of influence from the Old Testament and Judaism, and the theme of merit is developed much more powerfully. The author's attention is concentrated especially on the final decision at the last judgment (chs.23 and 26). Readiness for sacrifice is seen in the light of a competitive ideal, and the purple crown of martyrdom — which is not achieved by everyone — is contrasted with the white crown of good works, which anyone can attain. Like Tertullian and Clement of Alexandria before him, Cyprian rejects the 'love communism' of the early apostolic period, 'when . . . in the first beginnings the heart still proved to be alive in greater virtues and the faith of believers still glowed in a new warmth'. By holding goods in common, the first Christians imitated

> the equity of God the Father. For whatever is of God is common in our use,[2] nor is any one excluded from his benefits and his gifts, so as to prevent the whole human race from enjoying equally the divine goodness and liberality . . . In which example of equality, he who, as a possessor in the earth, shares his returns and his fruits with the fraternity, while he is common and just in his gratutitous bounties, is an imitator of God the Father (*De Op. et El.* 25).

Paul had already stressed the ideal of 'equality' (see p.39 above). Cyprian now bases it on God's attitude and demands 'imitation of God'. This idea — partly nourished from philosophical sources and partly from biblical sources — is to become especially significant with the great fathers of the fourth century (see above, pp.67f.). Cyprian does not question the legitimacy of private property any more than Clement and the later fathers, but he vigorously attacks the general misuse of it. Immediately after his baptism he is already depicting the great African property-owners with their insatiable desire for riches in a way which imitates Roman satire and his teacher Tertullian:

> They add forests to forests and, excluding the poor from their neighbourhood, stretch out their fields far and wide into space without any limits, possess immense heaps of silver and gold and mighty sums of money, either in built-up heaps or in buried stores, — even in the midst of their riches those are torn to pieces by the anxiety of vague thought, lest the robber should spoil, lest the murderer should attack, lest the envy of some wealthier neighbour should become hostile, and harass them with malicious lawsuits . . . From him there is no liberality to dependents, no communication to the poor. And yet such people call that their own money, which they guard with zealous labour, shut up at home as if it were another's . . .

Their possession amounts to this only, that they can keep others from possessing it: and oh, what a marvellous perversion of names! they call those things goods which they absolutely put to none but bad uses (*Ad Donat*.12).

This polemic against the anxiety and care which tempt men to accumulate riches and hope for everything from their possessions is also a constantly recurring theme of his later writing on good works:

If you dread and fear, lest, if you begin to act thus abundantly, your patrimony being exhausted with your liberal dealing, you may perchance be reduced to poverty: be of good courage in this respect, be free from care: that cannot be exhausted whence the service of Christ is supplied, whence the heavenly work is celebrated. Neither do I vouch for this on my own authority but I promise it on the faith of the Holy Scriptures and on the authority of the divine promise (*De Op. et El.*9).

Anyone who is so anxious about the way in which he is going to sustain his life that he does not trust this promise, 'that those who feed Christ are also in turn fed by Christ', is like those covetous Pharisees who mocked Jesus' parable of the unjust steward (Luke 16.1ff.,14). The claim to be concerned about children and family, or about the generations to come, is not a sufficient reason for not being generous. On the contrary,

the state neither takes away the property entrusted to God, nor does the exchequer intrude on it, nor does any forensic calumny overthrow it. That inheritance is placed in security which is kept under the guardianship of God ... You ... are sinning twice, both in not providing for your children the aid of God their Father, and in teaching your children to love their property more than Christ(ch.19, cf. 10.16-18).[3]

At a later date, Basil the Great (see above pp.2f.) laid special stress on the responsibility of those with property to abolish social injustice. He himself even sacrificed his own possessions to this end. He then brings up the influential idea of redistributing private property by means of legacies. The testator or the heir should make over a fixed part — Basil himself suggests half, on the basis of Luke 19.8 — to the poor. 'Strictly speaking, this conception of the "soul part" leads to a kind of church tax, a social tax for the struggle against poverty.'[4] Here too we find in the background the basic idea that God is the real master and owner of all possessions.

And so we come to a conclusion. The argument over the question of property, which already emerged in a radical way in the preaching of Jesus, was not settled in the early church, nor was there any clear and comfortable solution. The social demands associated with it introduced new stimuli to the ancient world which can be described without exaggeration as revolutionary. Of course the possibility of developing this new social ethic of agape and mutual equality was at first limited to Christian communities. The state was outside its range. Its sources were on the one hand Greek natural-law thinking and the ascetic ideal of self-sufficiency, and on the other the tradition of Old Testament prophecy and Jewish wisdom, though pride of place was of course taken by the impetus of the early Christian message itself. Even where the compromises demanded by historical circumstances were made, the intention of the early Christian message to act as a ferment continued to be effective. As a rule its foundation was explicitly theocentric. Even the natural-law arguments were drawn into this christologically determined 'theocentricity' and were changed as a result: God's graciousness, which takes shape in the work of Christ, liberates believers to do good with open hands, to overcome social barriers and to work for a just order.

The idea of merit, taken over from Judaism and to be found above all in Hermas, Tertullian or Cyprian, may be seen as a theological regression, but it was this that provided a strong motive for concrete social and philanthropic action. We may have had to subject this point to criticism, but we should not overlook the seriousness of its demands. Unlike some modern anthropologies, the fathers had no utopian, ideal picture of man; they knew that as a fallen creature man was selfish and a sinner by nature.

In many respects, an abyss separates us from the early church. But for that very reason we must try to see those things that still link us together, with the aim of making its spiritual and social life fruitful for our crisis-torn time.

12

Ten Concluding Theses

I shall attempt to indicate the possibilities of building the kind of bridge indicated in the previous chapter in ten theses:

1. We cannot extract a well-defined 'Christian doctrine of property' either from the New Testament or from the history of the early church. Right down to most recent times, views which have claimed to possess this character owe more to natural law than to Christianity. Where the beginnings of natural-law theories have been offered in the early church, whether for the purpose of radical criticism or to provide a relative justification for property, they have usually been borrowed from Graeco-Roman philosophical discussion. Of course they were closely associated with the biblical doctrine of creation.

2. By contrast, primitive Christianity contains a radical criticism of riches, a demand for detachment from the goods of this world and a conquest of the barriers between rich and poor through the fellowship of agape. All this comes about under the shadow of the imminent coming of the kingdom of God. It robs 'unrighteous mammon' of its force. In the further course of the history of early Christianity this stimulus leads to a tense controversy over injustice and the limitations and relative necessity of property.

3. Because they come from such a different situation, the various statements made in early Christianity can only be applied with many qualifications to our industrial society and the problems of possessions which so oppress us today. These

problems arise on the one hand from the progressive accumulation of productive capital and the concentration of economic power in the hands of relatively few people — including the state — and on the other from the irresistible transference to public corporations of the functions of care and protection hitherto bound up with possessions. Quite independently of the different and apparently antagonistic social systems, we find today that all over the world economic power and control is concentrated in the hands of a few 'functionaries' or élite groups.

4. By contrast, for the first Christians the question of property was a problem of personal ethics or at most the problem of relatively small groups. Their ethic was a theonomous community ethic, born of 'faith working through love'(Gal.5.6). The possibility of better social legislation by the state was no more within their scope than the limitation of the economic omnipotence of the state. A 'theocracy' which imposes the ideal of an allegedly divine will in the sphere of the state by means of political force is no more specifically Christian that the totalitarian 'philosophers' state', which seeks to justify itself on the basis of the sole rule of 'reason'.

5. As a result, early Christian ethics cannot provide us with any system of generally binding norms for today's society, nor does it set out to do so. However, we can gain certain insights from it which may hope to gain acceptance beyond the bounds of Christianity even today, especially as we can find some analogous notions in antiquity, sometimes even outside Christianity. One example is the idea that in some circumstances property leads man astray and puts him in danger, and that it can even seduce him into the misuse of power. Further, that for this very reason the misuse of power must be prevented by public controls and that those who own it must be obliged to use it also for the well-being of their fellow-men, or that a man's status and value in no way depend on his capacity to accumulate means of wealth. Readiness to refuse to become a consumer and to renounce luxury in a world in which extravagance and poverty often stand side by side can also very well be motivated by the Christian tradition.

6. Principles of this kind can have a considerable effect on the ethical conduct of both individuals and groups, and the perspicacious will gladly acknowledge their correctness. However, as a social ethic they will not make sufficient impact on society as a whole to solve the problems that face us to day. For § 14,2 of the Basic Law, 'Property confers obligations. Its use should at the same time serve the general good', is more the expression of a wish than of a norm proven in civic practice. In the Federal Republic, charitable foundations are still underdeveloped, tax evasion is partly regarded as a peccadillo, the placing of productive capacity in the hands of the workers is making all too slow process and public prestige is largely bound up with possessions. An egotistic private interest, oriented one-sidedly on consuming goods and increasing possessions, is holding back understanding of the urgent tasks which face the community: educational policies, protection of the environment, the improvement of the social structure for those who vegetate on the borders of our affluent society, and still more, of course, understanding of the problems of the Third World, and the poverty which is often increasing there rather than decreasing. This 'egotistic private interest' is to be found not only among individuals but in groups, associations, parties, trades unions and states, whose spheres of influence the individual can hardly avoid.

7. Here we can see a dilemma which we have already met in part, although in another form, in the discussion in early Christianity: the crisis of property also proves to be the crisis of man, his selfish desire to assert himself, his struggle for power and his mercilessness. Here we can see what the fathers called original sin. It may sound old-fashioned today, but it is very real.

8. Knowledge of man's selfish heart prevents the Christian from having an uncritical and utopian faith in the possibility of an ultimately perfect society, an infallibly political orthopraxy, a realizable ideal 'kingdom of freedom' which in some circumstances would have to be introduced by an act of force and whose goal would be the equality of all individuals and the end of 'man's rule over men'. Such 'equality' can

only be achieved through total manipulation and the utmost use of force. Like almost all philosophical utopian states, it leads to something very near to insect states. Moreover, as a rule what happens is that even more repressive ruling hierarchies take over the old structures. Man is not really equal, either in disposition and endowment, or in his wishes and needs. Equality must therefore be understood in the first place as real equality of opportunities, of the satisfaction of basic human needs. This equality is certainly progressing today in many democratic, free states with a concern for social justice, but in other parts of the world it is still far from being realized. The goal would be to grant each individual the chance of personal development in accordance with his capabilities and wishes, for the well-being of and in responsibility for the whole of society. The old opposition between freedom and righteousness can never be 'solved' except through a compromise.

9. This knowledge of man's selfish heart should not just lead to a resigned attitude which simply confirms and fixes existing social conditions. Precisely because man is entangled in his 'boundless' egotism both as an individual and as a group, we are called to constant reform, to progress towards the better. Eberhard Jüngel defines so-called 'progress' in history 'as progress in the reduction of an infinite series of ills'.[1] This also applies to the question of property. Because land and soil, pure air, water, energy and raw materials can no longer be 'produced' at will and thus there is a limit to industrial growth, new solutions must be found to the question. Of course we do not need new dualistic theories of society, but a readiness to prove what we have in social and economic reality, in which, in some circumstances, compromises may be required. Not least among these 'progressive' compromises is assent to the restriction of one-sided individual and collective 'rights' or 'privileges' in favour of the 'underprivileged' and the common good.

10. Finally, as an example of faith, we may remind ourselves of the attempt of the first Christian communities to resolve the tension which destroys fellowship between poor and rich, freemen and slaves, and to do away with opposi-

tions. This moves between the 'love communism' of the early community — which to our eyes seems unrealistic — and the more effective — but still endangered — compromise of the communities of the later period. This equalization created a healthy detachment from external goods, and at the same time overcame the barriers of status and class. The church, even today, could again become the place where mistrust and old prejudices are overcome and new forms of life and community are created on the basis of faith, love and hope. Furthermore, it is our duty as Christians and citizens to be ready to make sacrifices of our own and by pressure for better legislation break down social barriers, help minorities to achieve justice, and bring complexes of arbitrary power under better, democratic control. In this way we shall rob the 'demonic' nature of property of its force.

Bibliography

Chapter 1

In comparison with literature on the history of doctrine, relatively little has been written on the question of property or on the question of the social work of the early church. There is clear evidence here of the one-sidedness of Protestant patristic scholarship over the last decades. A brief survey of literature can now be found in W.-D. Hauschild, 'Christentum und Eigentum. Zum Problem eines altkirchlichen "Sozialismus" ', *ZEE* 16, 1972, 34-49 (34 n.2). Some earlier Catholic investigations are important, though of course they have a strongly apologetic character: I. Seipel, *Die wirtschaftsethischen Lehren der Kirchenväter* (Theologische Studien der Leo-Gesellschaft 18), Wien 1907; O. Schilling, *Reichtum und Eigentum in der altkirchlichen Literatur*, Diss., Tübingen/Freiburg 1908; id., 'Der Kollektivismus der Kirchenväter', *TQ* 114, 1933, 481-92; A. Bigelmair, 'Zur Frage des Sozialismus und Kommunismus der ersten drei Jahrhunderte', in *Festgabe Adolf Ehrhard*, Bonn 1922. The brief study by the Swiss Marxist Konrad Farner, *Christentum und Eigentum bis Thomas von Aquin*, Bern 1947, reprinted in the same author's *Theologie der Kommunismus*, Frankfurt 1969, 9-90, but without the detailed notes, is an idiosyncratic survey, but full of material. The penetrating study by S. Giet, *Les Idées et l'Action sociale de Saint Basile*, Paris 1941, 84ff., 96ff., 400ff. is specifically devoted to Basil the Great. In addition to the literature cited in Hauschild, mention should be made of: J. Leipoldt, *Der soziale Gedanke in der altchristlichen Kirche*, Leipzig 1950, reprinted 1972; K. Beyschlag, 'Christentum und Veränderung in der alten Kirche', *Kerygma und Dogma* 18, 1972, 26-55, esp.35ff.; H. Diessner, *Studien zur Gesellschaftslehre und sozialen Haltung Augustins*, Halle 1954; P. Christophe, *L'usage Chrétien du droit de Propriété dans l'Ecriture et la Tradition Patristique*, Paris 1963.

For early Christian charity and the social history of early Christianity, G. Uhlhorn, *Die christliche Liebestätigkeit in der alten Kirche*, Stuttgart 1882 (with indications of source material), and id., *Die christliche Liebestätigkeit*, Stuttgart ²1895 (reprinted Neukirchen 1959, without source material), are still indispensable; also A.von Harnack, *The Mission and Expansion of Christianity*, London 1908, reprinted New York 1961; E. Troeltsch, *The Social Teaching of the Christian Churches*, London 1931, two vols., reprinted New York 1960. C. Schneider, *Geistesgeschichte des antiken Christentums* I, Munich 1954, 504ff., 517ff.; W. Schwer, 'Armenpflege', in *Reallexikon für Antike und Christentum* I, 1950, 689ff. There is an urgent need for a social history of early Christianity. A very brief introduction is offered by E.A. Judge, *Christliche Gruppen in nichtchristlicher Gesellschaft*, 1964. An important study by H. Gülzow, 'Die sozialen Gegebenheiten der altchristlichen Mission', will soon appear in G. Kretschmar and H.-G. Frohnes (eds.), *Kirchengeschichte als Missionsgeschichte*.

For the social question in Graeco-Roman antiquity see the dated but still indispensable standard work R. v. Pöhlmann, *Geschichte der sozialen Frage und des Sozialismus in der antiken Welt*, revised and with an appendix by F. Oertel, Vols I and II, Munich [3]1925. Vol. II, 464ff., also deals with the early church. For criticism see J. v. Hasebroek, *Gnomon* 3, 1927, 257-66; also H. Bolkestein, *Wöhltätigkeit und Armenpflege im vorchristlichen Altertum*, Utrecht 1939 (reprinted Groningen 1967); J. Gagé, *Les Classes sociales dans l'Empire Romain*, Paris 1964; A. R. Hands, *Charities and Social Aid in Greece and Rome*, Ithaca, NY 1968. Unfortunately there is too brief a treatment of the Hellenistic period and of late antiquity, and the influence of Christianity is only mentioned on the periphery; N. Brockmeyer, *Socialgeschichte der Antike*, Urban-Taschenbücher 153, 1972. Quite essential for the whole economic and cultural background are the two standard works by M. Rostovtzeff, *The Social and Economic History of the Hellenistic World*, Vols. I-III, Oxford 1941, and *The Social and Economic History of the Roman Empire*, I and II, ed. P. M. Fraser, Oxford [2]1957.

For utopia in antiquity see, in addition to R. v. Pöhlmann (above), E. Salin, *Platon und die griechische Utopie*, Munich/Leipzig 1921; E. Nestle, *Vom Mythos zum Logos*, Stuttgart[2] 1942 (reprinted 1966), 462ff.; H. Braunert, *Utopia. Antworten griechischen Denkens auf die Herausforderung durch soziale Verhältnisse*, (Veröffentliehungen der schlesw.-holst. Universitätsgesellschaft, NF 51), Kiel 1969. A recent basic study is B. Gatz, *Weltalter, goldene Zeit und sinnverwandte Vorstellungen*, Hildesheim 1967. For the question of slavery see especially J. Vogt, *Sklaverei und Humanität*, [2]1972, esp. 20ff., 131ff.; C. Despotopoulos, 'La "Cité Parfaite" de Platon et l'Esclavage', *Revue des Etudes Grecques* 83, 1970, 26-37.

Chapter 2

For social order in the Old Testament see N. Peters, *Die soziale Fürsorge im Alten Testament*, 1935; F. Horst, *Das Eigentum nach dem AT* (1949), in id., *Gottes Recht*, Munich 1961; H. Donner, 'Die soziale Botschaft der Propheten im Lichte der Gesellschaftsordnung in Israel', *Oriens Antiquus* 2, 1963, 229-45; R. de Vaux, *Ancient Israel*, London 1961, 68ff., 80ff, 164ff.; H. H. Schmid, *Gerechtigkeit als Weltordnung*, Tübingen 1968; W. Zimmerli, *Man and his Hope in the Old Testament*, London 1971; M. Fendler, 'Zur Sozialkritik des Amos', *EvTh* 33, 1973, 32-53.

For Judaism see E. Bammel, 'Ptochos', *TDNT* VI, 894ff.; M. Hengel, *Judaism and Hellenism*, I London 1974, 6-57, 131ff., 175ff.; id., *Die Zeloten* (AGSU 1), Leiden 1961; A. Schalit, *König Herodes* (Studia Judaica 4), Berlin 1969, 256ff., 483.; H. Kreissig, *Die sozialen Zusammenhänge des judäischen Krieges* (Schriften zur Geschichte und Kultur der Antike 1), Berlin 1970.

For communal goods among the Essenes and in antiquity see W. Bauer, 'Essener', *Pauly-Wissowa*, Suppl. IV, 1924, 386-430 = *Aufsätze und kleine Schriften*, Tübingen 1967, 1-59 (esp. 19f., 33ff.); M. Hengel, *Judaism and Hellenism*, vol. I, 243ff.

For the social situation at the time of Jesus see E. Lohmeyer, *Soziale Fragen im Urchristentum*, 1921 (reprinted 1973); J. Jeremias, *Jerusalem in the Time of Jesus*, London 1969; M. Hengel, 'Das Gleichnis von den Weingärtnern Mc.12,1-12 im Lichte der Zenonpapyri und der rabbinischen Gleichnisse', *ZNW* 59, 1968, 1-39; id., *Victory over Violence*, Philadelphia 1973; M. Rostovtzeff, *Roman Empire* I, 261-73.

For rabbinic Judaism see H. Strack/P. Billerbeck, *Kommentar zum NT aus Talmud und Midrasch*, I, 1922, 817-28; IV, 1928, 536-610 (= Bill.).

Chapter 3

Jesus (and the NT): E. Lohmeyer, *Soziale Fragen im Urchristentum*; W. G. Kümmel, 'Der Begriff des Eigentums im Neuen Testament', *Heilsgeschehen und Geschichte*, (Marburger theologische Studien 3), 1965, 271-77; H.-J. Degenhardt, *Lukas, Evangelist der Armen, Besitz und Besitzverzicht in den lukanischen Schriften*, Stuttgart 1965; M. Hengel, *Was Jesus a Revolutionist?*, Philadelphia 1971; J. Jeremias, *New Testament Theology Vol. 1, The Proclamation of Jesus*, London 1971, 228f.; G. Breidenstein, *Das Eigentum und seine Verteilung*, Stuttgart/Berlin 1968, 288ff., lit.

Chapter 4

The early church: for Hellenistic style in Acts 2.22f. and 4.32 see E. Plumacher, *Lukas als hellenistischer Schriftsteller* (SUNT 9), Göttingen. 1972, 17ff.; K. Lake, 'The Communism of Acts II and IV-VI . . .', in F.J. Foakes Jackson/Kirsopp Lake, *The Beginnings of Christianity*, V, London 1932 (reprinted Grand Rapids 1966), 140-51; E. Haenchen, *The Acts of the Apostles*, Oxford 1971; H. Conzelmann, *Die Apostelgeschichte* (HNT 7), Tübingen 1963, 31, 38f.; E. Bloch, *Das Prinzip Hoffnung*, III, Stuttgart 1959, 1482-93; cf. also Seipel, *Der soziale Gedanke*, 107ff.; Lohmeyer, *Soziale Fragen in Urchristentum*, 79ff.

Chapter 5

Paul: Kümmel, 'Der Begriff des Eigentums'; W. Schrage, *Die konkreten Einzelgebote in der paulinischen Paränese*, Gütersloh 1961; id., 'Die Stellung zur Welt bei Paulus, Epiktet und in der Apokalyptik. Ein Beitrag zu I Kor.7.29-31', *ZThK* 61, 1964, 125-54; D. Georgi, *Die Geschichte der Kollekte des Paulus für Jerusalem.* (Theol.Forschung 38), Hamburg-Bergstedt 1965; O. Merk, *Handeln aus Glauben* (Marburger theol.Studien 5), 1968.

For the question of slavery in early Christianity see F. Bömer, *Untersuchungen zur Religion des Sklaven in Griechenland und Rom*, I-IV, Abh.Ak.Mainz 1957, 7; 1960, 4; 1961, 4; 1963, 10; H. Gülzow, *Christentum und Sklaverei*, Bonn 1969; J. Vogt, *Sklaverei und Humanität*. (Historia Einzelschriften 8), 1972.

Chapter 6

For the question of work and professions and organized social welfare
see A. v. Harnack, *The Mission and Expansion of Christianity*, London
1908 (reprinted New York 1961), 147-98; Leipoldt, *Der soziale
Gedanke*, 161ff.; Carl Schneider, *Geistesgeschichte* I, 693ff.; H.
Holzapfel, *Die sittliche Wertung der körperlichen Arbeit im christlichen
Altertum*, 1941.

Chapter 7

For the ascetic rejection of property see H. von Campenhausen, 'Early
Christian Asceticism', in id., *Tradition and Life in the Church*, London
1968, 90-122; G. Kretschmar, 'Ein Beitrag zur Frage nach dem
Ursprung der frühchristlichen Askese', *ZThK* 61, 1964, 27-67; P. Nagel,
Die Motivierung der Askese und der Ursprung des Mönchtums, (TU 95),
Berlin 1966; F. von Lilienfeld, 'Basilius der Grosse und die
Mönchsväter der Wüste', *ZDMG* Suppl. I, 2, 1969, 418-31. See also the
popular account of ancient monasticism and its rigorous asceticism in J.
Lacarrière, *The God-Possessed*, London 1963.

Chapter 8

For 'self-sufficiency' see P. Wilpert, 'Autarkie', *RAC* I, 1950, 1039-50.
Cf. R. Nickel, *Hermes* 100, 1972, 42-7. For the ideal of similarity to
God see H. Merki, *Homoiosis Theo*, Freiburg (Schweiz) 1952.

For the penetration of Christianity into the upper classes, A. von
Harnack, *Die Mission und Ausbreitung des Christentums*, Leipzig
[4] 1924, II, 559ff.; W. Eck, 'Das Eindringen des Christentums in den
Senatorenstand', *Chiron* I, 1971, 381-406. For the imitation of God see
A. Heitmann, *Imitatio Dei*, Rome 1940. For the Acts of Peter see E.
Hennecke—W. Schneemelcher—R. McL. Wilson, *New Testament
Apocrypha* II, London 1965, 259-321.

Chapter 9

For Marcion see A. von Harnack, *Marcion* [2] 1924, reprinted Darmstadt
1960.

Chapter 10

For Clement of Alexandria see H. von Campenhausen, *The Fathers of
the Greek Church*, London 1963, 25-36; H. Kraft, *Die Kirchenväter*,
Bremen 1966, 136-65; H. Lietzmann, *The Founding of the Church
Universal*, London [3] 1953, 277-94.

Chapter 11

For Cyprian see H. von Campenhausen, *The Fathers of the Latin
Church*, London 1964, 36-60; H. Kraft, *Die Kirchenväter*, 359-436; H.
Lietzmann, *The Founding of the Church Universal*, 225-38.

Abbreviations

Notes

Chapter 1

1. John Chrystostom, *Hom.XII on I Tim.4*: Migne, PG 62,563f.;
ET from NPNF, vol.XII, by Philip Schaff.
2. Cicero, *De Finibus*, 3,67; ET from LCL, by H. Rackham.
3. Gregory Nazianzen, *Hom.XIV,25*; Migne, PG 35, 892; cf. O.
Schilling, *Reichtum und Eigentum in der altkirchlichen Literatur*, Diss.,
Tübingen/Freiburg 1908.
4. Jerome, *De Officiis* I, 28: Migne, PL 16,67; ET from NPNF, by
H. de Romestin.
5. Aristophanes, *Ecclesiazousae* 590-4; ET from LCL, by B.B.
Rogers.
6. Ovid, *Metamorphoses* I, 89ff.; ET from LCL, by Frank Justus
Miller.
7. Virgil, *Georgics* 1, 126ff.; ET from LCL, by H. Rushton
Fairclough.
8. Strabo, *Geography* 7, 3, 9; ET from LCL, by Horace Leonard
Jones.

9.   Virgil, *Eclogues* 4, 39ff.; ET from LCL, by H. Rushton Fairclough.

10.   Seneca, *Ad Lucilium Epistulae Morales*; ET from LCL, by R.M. Gummere.

11.   Cf. B. Gatz, *Weltalter, goldene Zeit und sinnverwandte Vorstellungen*, Hildesheim 1967; cf. also F. Engels, *Der Ursprung der Familie, des Privateigentums und des Staats*, [4] 1891.

12.   Strabo, *Geography* 14,1,38; J. Vogt, *Sklaverei und Humanität*, [2] 1972, 31ff., 41ff.

13.   L. Koenen, *ZPapEp* 2, 1968, 205 line 44.

14.   W.W. Tarn, *Cambridge Ancient History* VII, 741ff.

15.   E. Plumacher, *Lukas als hellenistischer Schriftsteller*, SUNT 9, Göttingen 1972, 17f.

16.   H. Chadwick, *The Sentences of Sextus*, Cambridge University Press 1959, no.278.

17.   M. Dibelius and H. Conzelmann, *The Pastoral Epistles*, Philadelphia 1972, 85f.; see below, p.000.

18.   See Polycarp 4; Tertullian, *De Patientia* 7,5; Clement of Alexandria, *Paedagogus* 2,39,3, cf. 38,5.

19.   Cf. C. Spicq, *Les Epîtres Pastorales* I, Paris [4] 1969, 564; W.F. Arndt — F.W. Gingrich — W. Bauer, *A Greek-English Lexicon of the New Testament*, Chicago 1957, 866.

20.   Pseudo-Phocylides 41; Sib.3,235f., 642f.; 8,17f. and often in Philo.

21.   Menander, *Dyskolos*, frag.; ET from LCL by Francis G. Allinson, 345f.

22.   H. Hommel, in *Festschrift zum 65. Geburtstag Walter Mönch*, Heidelberg 1971, 20ff.

Chapter 2

1.   Otto Kaiser, *Isaiah 1-12*, OTL, London and Philadelphia 1972, 70.

2.   K. Elliger, *Leviticus*, HAT 4, Tübingen 1966, 356.

3.   M. Hengel, *Victory over Violence*, Philadelphia 1973, 32; id., *Die Zeloten* (AGSU 1), Leiden 1961, 341f.

4.   M. Hengel, *Judaism and Hellenism*, Vol. I, London and Philadelphia 1974, 036ff.

5.   4QpPs 37 II, 9ff.; ET from G. Vermes, *The Dead Sea Scrolls in English*, Harmondsworth [2] 1965, 243f.

6.   1 QM 11.8f., 13; ET from Vermes, op.cit., 138.

7.   Tos.Pea 4,19 = Sukka 49b; Bill.4,537, cf. 541.

8.   Bab. Keth.50a; Bill.4,550f.

9.   Keth.110b; Sanh.100b; cf. E. Bammel, *TDNT* VI, 901.

10.   Pes.R.Kah. 1,241f., ed. Mandelbaum; Hag. 9b, etc.

Chapter 3

1.   W.G. Kümmel, 'Der Begriff des Eigentums im Neuen Testa-

ment', *Heilsgeschehen und Geschichte*, Marburger Theologische Studien 3, 1965, 271-7.

   2.   Jerome, *Ep*.120,1,11: Migne, PL 22, 985; cf. R. von Pöhlmann, *Geschichte der Sozialen Frage und des Sozialismus in der antiken Welt* II, Munich [3] 1925, 470.

Chapter 4

   1.   Ernst Bloch, *Das Prinzip Hoffnung* III, Stuttgart 1959, 1488.

Chapter 6

   1.   Cyprian, *Ep*.2.2; ET from ANF, by A. Cleveland Coxe, Vol.V, 356, where it is numbered *Ep*.60.
   2.   Eusebius, HE 4,23,10; ET from H.J. Lawlor and J.E.L. Oulton, *Eusebius: The Ecclesiastical History*, SPCK 1927, 130.
   3.   A. von Harnack, *The Mission and Expansion of Christianity in the First Three Centuries* I, Williams and Norgate 1908, 158f.
   4.   Harnack, op.cit., 171ff.

Chapter 7

   1.   R. von Pöhlmann, *Geschichte der Sozialen Frage* I[3], 492.
   2.   'Christian Sibyllines', in: E. Hennecke — W. Schneemelcher — R. McL. Wilson, *New Testament Apocrypha* II, Lutterworth Press 1965, 718, translated by R. McL. Wilson. The passage is Sib.2,318-24.
   3.   M. Krause and P. Labib, *Gnostische und Hermetische Schriften aus Cod.II and Cod.VI*, 107ff., cf. *ThLZ* 98, 1973, 13ff.
> 4.   Op.cit., 11f.
   5.   Tertullian, *Apologia* 39.10f., cf. *Ep.Diogn*.5.7f.
   6.   Minucius Felix, *Octavius* 36,5; ET from ANF, by A. Cleveland Coxe.
   7.   Acts of Thomas 20, in *New Testament Apocrypha* II, 453; cf. chs.62,96,136, pp.477,493,514.
   8.   Ibid., chs.144f., p.519.
   9.   Ibid., ch.45, p.468; ch.47, p.469.
  10.   Ibid., ch.37, pp.463f.; cf. ch.117, p.505.
  11.   Ibid., chs 60,100, pp.476,494.
  12.   Ibid., ch.66, p.479; cf. chs.83-85, pp.487f.
  13.   Ibid., ch.59, p.475.
  14.   Ibid., ch.164, p.522.
  15.   Ibid., chs. 131,170, pp.512,531.
  16.   P. Nagel, *Die Motivierung der Askese und der Ursprung des Mönchtums*, (TU 95), Berlin 1966, 34ff., 75ff.

Chapter 8

   1.   M. Hengel, *Nachfolge und Charisma* (BZNW 34), Göttingen 1968, 32.
   2.   A. Resch, *Agrapha, Aussercanonische Schriftfragmente gesam-*

melt und untersucht, Leipzig ²1906, no.171, pp.198f.; cf. above, p.5l1
3.   H. Chadwick, *The Sentences of Sextus*, 160.
4.   Ibid., 87.
5.   Clement of Alexandria, *Paedagogus* 2,128,2; cf. 1,98,4; *Strom.* 3,89; 6,24,8, and below pp.74ff.

Chapter 9

1.   Lucian, *Peregrinus* 13; ET from LCL V, by A.M. Harmon.
2.   *Didascalia Apostolorum* 13; ET from ibid., *The Syriac Version translated and accompanied by the Verona Fragments* by R. Hugh Connolly, Clarendon Press 1929. Cf. Harnack, *The Mission and Expansion*, 177ff.
3.   *New Testament Apocrypha* II, 98,
4.   A. von Harnack, *Marcion*, Berlin 1921, 24ff.
5.   Ch.18, *New Testament Apocrypha* II, 300.
6.   Ch.22, ibid., 304.
7.   Ch.30, ibid., 314.
8.   Harnack, *The Mission and Expansion*, 157f.
9.   H. Gülzow, *Christentum und Sklaverei*, Bonn 1969, 142-72; there is an English text of the relevant part of the Refutation in J. Stevenson, *A New Eusebius*, SPCK 1957, 160ff.
10. Gülzow, op.cit., 165.
11. Ibid., 172.

Chapter 10

1.   *Hist.Aug.*29,85f. = Fl.Vopiscus, *Vita Sat.*
2.   Clement of Alexandria, *Paedagogus* 2,119,2-120,5; cf. *Protrept.* 122,3; ET from ANF, by A. Cleveland Coxe, which is also used for the other extracts from Clement.

Chapter 11

1.   Cf. *Vita* 15, and H. Kraft, *Die Kirchenväter*, Bremen 1966, 362f.
2.   *Quodcumque enim Dei est in nostra usurpatione commune est*, cf. Ambrose and Cicero, above, pp.3f.
3.   ET here and in this chapter from ANF, by A. Cleveland Coxe.
4.   W.-D. Hauschild, *ZEE* 16, 1972, 45.

Chapter 12

1.   Eberhard Jüngel, *Unterwegs zur Sache*, Tübingen 1972,272.